DISCOVER THE SECRET
ENTREPRENEUR IN YOU

THE
GUY
WHO FIRED HIS
BOSS

TURN YOUR SIMPLE IDEA
INTO A THRIVING BUSINESS

DISCOVER THE SECRET
ENTREPRENEUR IN YOU

THE
GUY
WHO FIRED HIS
BOSS

TURN YOUR SIMPLE IDEA
INTO A THRIVING BUSINESS

SAM KARIUKI

Published by Sahel Publishing Association,
a subsidiary of Sahel Books Inc.
P.O. Box 18007—00100
Nairobi, Kenya
Tel: +011-254-715-596-106
For questions and orders log on to:
www.WeMakeSellingEasy.net
www.TheGuyWhoFiredHisBoss.com

A Sahel Book
Nairobi. New Delhi. London. Nashville.
Editor: Sam Okello
Interior design by Hellen Wahonya Okello
Cover by: Joan Chizi
Cover Arranged by: Hellen Wahonya Okello
Printed in India

To Terry, My beloved!

ACKNOWLEDGEMENT

No book is ever the product of one person's wisdom and intelligence. This is one is no exception. I may not mention everyone who has made contributions to bringing this dream to a success, but whether you are mentioned or not, I appreciate you.

First is to my life partner, Terry, without whose support and encouragement my entrepreneurial journey would have never started. Jeremy, Michelle and Tatiana—my children who give me the motivation to do all I need to do to succeed.

Thank you, Tom Wanyonyi, for challenging me to put my thoughts into a book and enduring the pain of reading the raw first draft. My special friends: Steve Wachira , Jeff Ngotho and Henry Owaga, for holding me accountable. Margaret, my first business partner, the lessons we learnt are in the book.

Marion Wakahe, whose feedback gave the book the form it has taken. Salome, my editor, for hard work and advice. Didi, Dorcas and Kendi, my marketing assistant; your support has been immense.

All my clients, without whom I would not have a story to write. Special mention to Brian Muthiani , George Rabala, Edward Njoroge, Tasleem Abdulla, Nene Kalinga, Charity Ndegwa and Anne Kiarie.

Sam and Hellen Okello, of Sahel Publishing Association, and your entire team. You are amazing. The final product that people are enjoying was cooked by you.

Everyone reading this book—you made me write it. Thank you!

My heartfelt gratitude to God, who not only gave me the desire, but the health, strength and resources to make it happen. You brought me many people and ideas without which this book would have never been.

FOREWORD

Having an idea is easy; turning it into a business is the hard part. In my business life I've come across people who talk of ideas they had, but which never transitioned into business. I've also seen people who jumped in with an idea without giving it proper testing—before burning their money. Both of these tendencies leave a lot of regret and pain in life, not to mention the material losses such can cost those who are close to us.

Whereas there are many books and resources on how to manage businesses, there are few that help the entrepreneur get to build a business to a level that would require that management. Many entrepreneurs, who are starting out, grope in the dark, with a lot of trial and error, some succeed but a majority never succeed. Those who fail either quit their entrepreneurial endeavors altogether or imagine that all they need is to make another try to succeed. That is a tragedy many entrepreneurship courses have not addressed.

This book is a focused attempt at providing a structure into entrepreneurship endeavors for new businesses and even for existing ones seeking to venture into new areas. Successful entrepreneurs, just like successful people in other aspects of life, don't come in one colour, size or shape, but there are a few things you will find common in them regardless of their education level, life exposure or work experience: they follow simple processes that deliver the results needed.

Reading through this book one finds a process that any person can follow and turn his or her idea into a business. There are tools one can use to assess how good their idea is as well as an easy-to-follow process to plan the business—which the writer calls *business design*. This is a process that I wish I had access to in my early days in entrepreneurship. I would have saved myself many days and money. I believe in reading. I read widely on all aspects of business. When you have read many books it becomes harder and harder to come across a book that stands out. The book Sam has written is one of the outstanding ones. It is heavy in business wisdom, but very easy read. The business novel approach is refreshingly new, especially for Africa.

If you are a busy person struggling to find time to read complex materials that could transform your life, this book is it! Appropriately titled *The Guy Who Fired His Boss,* you will find in it interesting phrases that make the understanding of complex ideas easy. You may not pass a business exam if you adopt some of Sam's fascinating definitions, but you will pass the exam of success in the *real* entrepreneurial world—which is that place he calls *the businesses trenches.*

Sam is the right person to write this book. I say so because my company has engaged Sam as a business growth consultant and trainer for the last two years and every shilling we have paid for his services has paid back many times over. Unlike other consultants, he is willing to be held accountable for results. I believe he does the same with the concepts shared in this book. At whatever stage you are in the entrepreneurial journey – aspiring, practicing or veteran – you will find this book worth your money and time.

Edward Njoroge
Founder & CEO
Track & Trace

PREFACE

Just about everyone you meet has harbored aspirations of starting a business sooner or later in life. That aspiration comes from the desire to make more money, to be free from an employer, to pursue a childhood dream or just to do something that ushers variety into their life. While most people may never come to a point where they act on these aspirations, others will find a way to make a dive into the sea of entrepreneurship.

This sea's waters are bloodied by the death of many new businesses that were started by men and women driven by great intentions. Those who are strong-willed will keep on making the plunge until one day they survive, while a majority will learn from the painful losses they incurred and never try again.

We could presume that those who succeed in starting and building successful businesses were either born entrepreneurs, who whatever they touch turns to gold, while others may have been lucky to be at the right place at the right time. But when you spend time with those who succeed and those who failed, you will soon discover that what made the difference was not so much in who they were, but how they did it.

This book is intended to help you understand this very point. It helps you discover how to convert your great idea into a great business. So whether you are an experienced or a newbie entrepreneur you will find this book insightful. The book will inspire those who are scared to start the journey; encourage those who are struggling to make their new businesses work; and be helpful to those who would just enjoy studying the art and science of entrepreneurship.

While writing this book, I kept my son in mind and hoped it would make sense to him by the time he turned ten. I don't pretend to be an originator of the ideas contained in this book, but I have sought to simplify and make practical critical elements that make successful entrepreneurship. After reading to the end, you will be the judge of whether I have succeeded in this mission or not.

The book has been written in the novel format for two key reasons. One, when crafting the book as a story I was forced to make the book as simple as possible without diluting the intended wisdom to be shared. Two, of course, was to help you find it easy to follow and tie together the various points made in the book. Stories are powerful and memorable. If you connect with the great story shared in this book you will be a better entrepreneur.

My primary motivation for writing this book *is* a deep desire to foster the development and equipping of entrepreneurs—those who will make the right choices and create successful enterprises while minimizing unnecessary pain and suffering many experience.

But there is a difference between *a primary motivation* and *a main reason*. The main reason I wrote is to raise funds to reduce the suffering that so many people in Kenya are going through as a result of cancer. I lost my mother to cancer two years ago and I promised myself I would do something to shield others from going through what Mama went through.

At the time of writing this introduction I am from the Kenyatta National Hospital to help my uncle get booking for radiotherapy treatment. While there, I met people from all regions of this country; people from all income levels; people of all ages—all desperate for the little that this hospital can offer. From what I saw, it is sad to say not many of them will see the beginning of their treatment. They will travel back home in pain, staring at an uncertain future. I want to see the end of this. I will do my small part to end it. My small part is writing this book. Your small part is buying this book. Part of the proceeds will go towards easing the suffering caused by cancer among the people living in the informal settlements of Kenya. Enjoy the reading!

TABLE OF CONTENT

CHAPTER 1

TILL BUSINESS DO US PART

"I'm fed up, John, can't take this anymore," Michelle screamed from the bedroom. The outburst of anger gave way to a cry of deep anguish. "I cannot be a mother, a father and the sole provider for this family. I'm done!" Her fury was directed at the helpless red suitcase in which she was frantically packing her children's clothes. She wanted to get out of her marriage of five years right now—not a second longer. She'd had it with John.

John had struggled to put food on the table. He was a brilliant man, who had quit his job to start a business, but since that promising start, four years of his entrepreneurial exploits had passed and the lowest ebb was fast approaching to coincide with his fifth year of marriage. Things were neither going right at home nor in business and he feared he was the reason for the dramatic collapse of his marriage—even if his decision to go into business had been well intentioned.

From the onset the business never generated money to meet the basic needs of the family. Michelle had had to take care of the family bills and on many occasions took care of her husband's needs as though he were one of her children. She had done it gladly, for many months; hoping things would take the path of John's dreams. But her husband's upbeat assessment of the future led to spiraling and crippling debt and the family sank into deeper hopelessness with each upbeat assessment.

Just the other day, the fuming landlord had asked them to vacate the apartment unit they had lived in for five years by close of the day. Michelle had promised to get a loan to clear the rent arrears, which had softened the landlord's heart. He had reluctantly agreed to hold off on confiscating their household goods. The loan was to be in addition to other debts she had already incurred, including one she had taken from Jahazi Sacco (a cooperative society) to finance her husband's business.

After the landlord incident, John had sat on the floor. He had not slept a wink all night. He had thought of how he could salvage his marriage, but he had run out of options. What hurt him most was that the kids knew there was trouble. They no longer talked to him as they usually did. This hurt him deeply and he spent many waking hours wondering what he could do to turn around the situation. He knew he had to do something fast or it would be too late.

He was a good man with good intentions—a man with dreams of prosperity for his family, but being a good man, as he was now finding out, was not sufficient to firmly glue a marriage. And neither could good intentions pay rent. Only money could!

"This crap of being an entrepreneur is not working for anyone. It has not worked in the last five years. It will never work," Michelle said between sobs.

Her heaving husband wanted to hold her as he had done before, but he sensed it was the wrong thing to do. Michelle's mind was made up. She was leaving!

She said, "Stop being lazy! Be a man! Get a job, John!"

John finally looked down. He was heartbroken. He felt a violent stub of pain in his heart as it occurred to him he was separating from children he really loved. He had struggled to be there for them—financially and otherwise—but his dream had run into a gray brick wall. It now saddened him, as he caught himself admit, that maybe it was for the better that Michelle left with the children. *Maybe they'll be better-off without me!*

"When you figure out how to be a father, John, you can look for us," Michelle said as she led her two kids to a pickup that was ready to roar off with the family's belongings. "Bye, John!"

As Michelle led the children away, John recalled an incident a few weeks ago. On that warm afternoon, the older son had asked for marshmallows. Before John could answer his first son with *There is no money right now, but I will buy you marshmallows for sure*, the second son cut him short and said, "Dad, I know marshmallows are expensive, but God will give you money!"

Those sharp words had cut deep and meant a lot, but God had not given him any money. The little that had come his way he had borrowed from friends.

John wished he had listened to his wife when she first advised him to close down the business, but he had felt too close to the dream to give up. She had pointed to many facts, warning that being in business was a bad idea for a family man, but John had placed his faith in a simple formula. It was this:

Great Idea + Hard Work = Fat Bank Account

It was that fat bank account, the endless possibilities it offered his family, that drove John. He wanted Michelle and the children to lack nothing. He was motivated by love, not adventure; security for the future, not juvenile gamesmanship. Now his dream was in ruins. What was he going to do? Where would he start to pick up the pieces? He wobbled back into the bare living room and collapsed on the floor. Right there, the banks of his stream of tears broke. They flooded the floor!

———

A couple of hours after Michelle left, John went to the bedroom and sat on the bare floor as he reflected on some of Michelle's words: *You are not Donald Trump, so forget it with your nice guy demeanor. You are too laid back for business.*

Those words, as they swam like a gentle wave through his mind, hurt John so much, but he also knew there was truth in them. He was not the go-getter Trump was. He was John!

Utterly defeated, John now longed for death. He talked to God as to a friend and said, "Why me, God? Kill me or I'll do it myself!"

God didn't answer.

In his torturous anguish, John cried himself to sleep like a three-month-old baby who had been abandoned by the mother. He was later woken up by the ringing of his phone. It was a strange number. He hoped it was not any of his creditors, who was using a different line to get in touch. He had not been answering their calls the last couple of weeks, having run out of promises to blunt their anger. He had simply ignored their calls.

But now there was no time to waste. John needed to leave the house immediately. The new occupant had to move in this very morning and John knew he had to get going, but he needed courage to leave. The caretaker, the house girls, the guards and all the housewives had congregated to bask in the sweet morning sun. They were catching up on the happenings in his house.

He had projected his family as a perfect one, but he knew his house girl and the gossipy caretaker had burst that image. He watched with embarrassment as people talked animatedly and laughed as they looked at his house. He could not hear what they said, but he knew they were talking about him and how he had been abandoned by his wife. Finally coming to grips with the inevitability of the moment, he threw the few clothes he had in his son's school bag—which had been left by mistake—and got ready to depart.

But how was he going to leave the house in the full glare of the neighborhood journalists? He felt naked and totally exposed. He came to understand why people, caught up in silly situations, covered their eyes and faces from the cruelty of the camera and the merciless stares of gossipers.

As he finally opened the door and came face to face with the neighborhood journalists, he recalled a line he always used whenever he saw people caught up in a mess. The line was this: *Everyone goes down at some point.* But this morning he added a new line: *It is what you do to get up that makes the difference!*

The phone began to ring again as he came down the stairs. It was the same number. "It can't get any worse," he whispered to himself and answered it.

CHAPTER 2

THE GUY WHO FIRED HIS BOSS

Sleeping on a sofa, in his younger brother's house, was tough. A lot went through John's mind. The sofa hurt his back and further injured his already bruised ego. A man's ego is his most prized possession. When it is wounded, it takes ages to heal.

But John had to do what he had to. He was discovering, and fast, what it was to be a *true* husband and father. He was waking up to the troubling reality that as a father and husband he should not have done what he loved and was passionate about, but what was good for his family.

Coming up on his lazy elbow and yawning away the sleepless night, John kicked down the blanket and got himself spruced up in less than ten minutes. He needed to make it to the interview on time—and there was no Michelle to help prep him or fix the tie and jacket. He was on his own. Life had reduced him to loneness again and he knew it was his fault.

Since resigning from his job to go into business, John had never imagined himself employed again. He had been offered many jobs along the way, but had passed them up without as much as second thoughts. He had remained steadfast in self-employment in spite of the alluring perks some companies offered.

That fiery resolve had finally collapsed after Michelle's departure just yesterday. He was excited by a chance at another job. If he got it, the job could enable him to get back on track and take care of his family again. It could also save him the damning indignity of being housed by his younger brother and his friends, who were trying to get their life started after leaving college. The boys had looked up to him and had all along aspired to start their own businesses, to be like him, but now they were not too sure business was such a great idea. His current circumstances did not support this advice; if anything he needed to free them to think about pursuing jobs before the market got flooded.

His motivation for venturing into entrepreneurship was to be free from his irritating boss, to be free to do what he loved best. Getting into business was, thus, John's declaration of independence.

Five years ago *I Fired My Boss* was his life's organizing principle. He uttered the words whenever and wherever he introduced himself. On many such occasions, people complemented him for his courage. He even felt pity for his many graduate friends, who were what he termed *Corporate Slaves*. People even started calling him The Guy Who Fired His Boss!

But now John was looking forward to rejoining that derided slavery. He was desperate to hire a boss, or be hired by one. The trouble was—John had never applied for a job in years. Michelle had done it for him. She had done it without his consent or knowledge. She had felt her husband needed a job, but was too stubborn to admit or realize it. Acting out of pure pragmatism, she had written and broadcasted his resume to those who were interested and those who were not.

"Just get John a job, any job!" she had told her friends. In her opinion, the man needed to be saved from his delusion that he was in business. She often referred to his business as creative idling. She never told him what she was doing to help, but some of her girlfriends' men mentioned it to him.

But even after John got to know what Michelle was up to he never asked her to stop. He appreciated her efforts, never letting her know he felt they were inspired by foolishness. Whenever he was shortlisted for an interview he politely turned it down. Ironically, one of those very applications had resulted in a job opportunity this morning. He was, at last, silently thankful for what his wife had done all along to avoid a breakup.

Due to the deflating drama of the previous day, John had not prepared for the interview. What he lacked in preparation, however, he made up for in appearance. His brother's grey suit, white shirt and maroon tie were good for his 5'7" frame and dark complexion. He felt strange in the formal clothes, but he also knew it was little things like clothes one wore, and their colours, that made a difference in events of that nature.

John heard a voice:

> "You are making a big mistake. After coming this far, why quit now?"

The voice was compelling and relentless, but he ignored it even though he felt the urge to agree with it.

Walking out of his business now would confirm that he was a failure. He had resisted his parents' and relatives' pressure to hold a job. They had considered him too intelligent, and too highly educated, to be in the Jua Kali sector, working without the assurance of a stable pay.

"This hustling thing should be left to those of us who never made it to college," one of the uncles told him even though his life needed more help than John's. He went on to tell John how he would regret his decision. Looking back now, John shuddered at the thought of having to prove his uncle's prophecy true. *If I get this job I will make it a big secret*, he swore.

John knew he could not lose by being too early, but he could by being a bit late. The interview was scheduled for 8:00 a.m. One hour before then, he was seated at the visitors' lounge. He repeatedly and unconsciously took deep breaths as he waited. That calmed his nerves. He felt close to getting a job as the hour wore down. After the job, getting back his family was the next priority and now he felt only minutes separated him from a tearful reunion with his wife and children.

Getting the job would prove to Michelle that he loved her and the kids so much; that he was ready to do a thing he so hated for their sake. That sacrifice was the clearest indication that he had evolved into a real father and husband, he thought.

In his mind, he went through the various business debts and problems this job would help him escape: unpaid office rent and pending salaries, nagging clients, unproductive employees, unresolved and unresolvable disagreements with clients… Just a job and he would be a new man!

A smile formed.

Just then, a metallic black Mercedes Benz drove into the compound. It looked like the ones usually deployed in the presidential convoy. He admired it, but was quick to warn himself that he would never drive such a machine if he got this job. But even from his business the imposing car would have only remained a tantalizing dream unless he had landed a lucrative government project through corrupt means. He thought the owner of the machine must have acquired it through such means.

As the car crawled to a smooth stop, the guards saluted. John was not sure whether it was the occupants they saluted or the car. His mind came back to the interview. The most common question asked was: tell us about yourself. It was 7:55 a.m.

Tell us about yourself. He heard the question replay in his mind. He dreaded it. As he had sat in the speeding *matatu*, he had rehearsed his answer:

> I was born in Kajiado County thirty five years ago. I went to school there—both primary and secondary education. I later joined the University of Nairobi. I studied business administration and graduated with first class honours degree. After graduating, I got a job with Web Guru, the largest web design firm in Kenya at the time. I worked for seven years. I rose through the ranks from a sales executive to the head of web design services. Later, I went on to found E-Biz Solutions. I have been running the firm for the last five years and we have been privileged to

> serve various respectable organizations. I'm
> loyal, I'm self-driven and I'm highly disciplined.
> Whatever I set my mind on, I give my all. These
> are the traits that have brought me this far.

He felt that such answer would impress any employer
and it brought him a measure of calm.

But what if the question he dreaded most and had safely
pushed away from his mind was asked. Fearing it just
might pop up, he rehearsed it:

> John, you left formal employment for business.
> Now you want to leave self-employment for
> formal employment. Why?

John did not have an answer. He had read somewhere
that employers found it hard to hire people who had
been self-employed for too long. Such people, they
feared, did not stay in jobs and on seeing new business
opportunities, left. He knew that was not true. Those
who had been rescued by a job, from a failing business,
rarely went back to self-employment. Their will was
completely broken. Like them, he was not going back to
business if he got this job. His mind was made up.

"John Juma?" It was a lady's voice.

John got up and followed her. She gave him direction to
the interviewer's room. He could hear his heart pound.

He knocked gently on the door. An elderly man, of Asian descent, stood to welcome him. He seemed to be in his early seventies. As he invited John to take a seat, he handed him his business card.

John stared at the card. He thought he was dreaming. He knew the man owned the business, but he had never expected to be interviewed by the owner himself.

CHAPTER 3

BURSTING HOPES IN SIXTY MINUTES

⁕

This is a man John admired greatly but had never met other than on a few brief appearances on the local media. John had read every article of his that he had come across. If it was not for the business card, John could not have imagined this was him. He was smaller than John had imagined him to be. He was also easy going and had a reassuring presence. John had feared that this industrial magnet was an egotistical beast like all multibillionaires were—at least that's what he'd thought of them. He was now learning that if indeed multibillionaires were egotistical, there were some who were not; like the man he was with right now.

The Asian led a quiet, private life. His rise to great wealth and business success remained a mystery. He was not connected to big families and political operatives like most people of a similar net worth. Such an enigma he was that people created simplistic theories around his success. He never tried to set the record straight, though, perhaps because he saw no value in such a venture; and he may have even come to the conclusion that such speculation was good for business.

The few times the media interviewed him they only published stories around his work.

In an article that John had read in the country's leading newspaper, V.J. Shah was described as the greatest, living industrialist in the country. They wrote of how an orphan boy rose to great wealth through hard work and determination. This was only mentioned in a few sentences. The writer was more interested in revealing the profile of V.J. as one of the wealthiest people in the country.

Another publication that followed this article ran the headline to V.J.'s story thus: *The Compassionate Capitalist.* It did this as it covered, in dramatized detail, his philanthropic initiatives across the country.

Other than his chain of supermarkets, people knew little of what other businesses he owned. His firms were mainly in industrial chemicals and plastics. This factory complex, where they were now, was one of the smallest of those firms, but it was the one that housed his personal office. It manufactured food-packaging materials for the export market.

"I want you to make this decision quickly," V.J. said as he concluded the so called interview. It had lasted sixty minutes. It was a conversation. A conversation John could not have expected. Sixty minutes that left him worse off than when he had arrived for the interview. If he had any more tears remaining in his reserve tank, he could have shed more; but he hadn't any left!

The emotional cocktail of anger, confusion, and sadness brewed inside. Why raise his hopes so high then crash them, he wondered. Why did V.J. do that to him?

He hadn't wanted a job. He had never applied for one. At a point of desperation, he had come to the interview. But V.J. had not only wasted his time, he had made his life more complicated. He had made a crazy proposition to him and had wanted immediate response. In negotiations you are advised to look for an excuse that buys you time to think through a matter and gather new information before making a stupid decision. John lied that he needed to consult his wife!

"It is in the character of great business people to make decisions quickly, John," V.J had said.

But John hated quick decisions. Probably Michelle was right in her assessment of his incapacity to excel as an entrepreneur. Quick leads to bad decisions, he feared.

John was now at the same point he was before this so called interview—without his wife, children and with no way out of his financial woes. These were the cards life had dealt him. These were the cards he had to play with. It had come down to that.

He needed to fight. He was in a war that had only one outcome to look forward to: winning. The alternative was shame, ridicule and loss of his cherished family forever. The only consolation he had was that he knew most entrepreneurs had to face these moments before they got their big break. He also knew many others never get to see that big break.

CHAPTER 4

THE SALVATION THAT WAS NOT

John stood at the busy Kampala Road bus stop amid a large crowd of commuters. All the buses charged more than he could afford. He was not alone. No one was boarding because the charge was ten shillings more than the usual fare. But this was not unusual for him. It was common for many entrepreneurs, when they were down, to experience such pains. They found themselves without cash to facilitate moving around to deliver goods and services, attend sales meetings or even do something as needful as collecting cheques. Such a low season required tenacity. Giving up led to missing out on opportunities. Persistent folks like John did whatever they had to do. Many times that meant walking. From the bus stop, John could see Kenyatta International Conference Centre so he could walk to town. This was a manageable distance. Walking, after all, was healthy, cheaper and therapeutic. It also reduced his carbon footprint. The walk would afford him time to think through V.J.'s strange proposition.

He joined many others who had opted to walk. It was the only alternative they had. Most of them had come early morning seeking casual work in various factories. Walking at this time of the day meant they were the unlucky ones. The lucky ones would take the walk later in the evening, after the day's labour was done. Such was life for those who come every day to Industrial Area looking for work.

As they walked, John overheard stories of sick parents, kids who were at home for lack of school fees, locked houses by landlords, empty food jars...

He also learnt that some of these people were starting out the 'hustling life' in the city. They were hosted by relatives, hopefully for a short while as they sought employment. They were a curious mixture of skilled and unskilled, schooled and unschooled folks. They all hoped the following day would turn out better.

John wished he could do something urgently to liberate humanity from the scourge of joblessness. This was every entrepreneur's burden—creating opportunities for others to meet their needs.

But on this day he was walking to town with them, facing the very same predicament as them. The only difference between him and them was that he was better dressed. The walk was longer than he had projected. He slowly drifted back to minding his business.

He recalled V.J.'s story of how he had lost his parents as a child. The father was mauled by the wicked man eaters of Tsavo. He was a rail construction worker. To most people, the story of lions and how they feasted on Indian rail workers was merely an entertaining story in school textbooks; but for V.J. it was a personal tragedy.

Then V.J.'s mother died shortly after her husband's death. It was malaria that claimed her life. This was the main motivation behind his contribution in initiatives intended to reduce deaths caused by malaria in East Africa. He wanted to wipe out malaria if he could.

Later, a compassionate couple, one that did not have children of their own, took V.J. to be their only son. The couple ran a small shop at that time, which latter grew to become the much revered Indian Ocean Mega Stores, a distribution and wholesale chain.

V.J. enrolled in school, but never went beyond primary school. After dropping out, he assisted his foster parents in the shop. He learnt a lot about business from observing how Rajiv managed and grew the shop.

Rajiv Shah, V.J.'s adoptive father, spent evenings explaining to V.J. the reason behind his actions and decisions and how they contributed to the success of the business. Rajiv was always very intentional in how he ran the shop. He never allowed emotions, good or bad, to influence his business decisions. Rajiv called his entrepreneurship model *common sense*.

"Without this education, I would not have known what to do in business," V.J. had told John.

After V.J. turned sixteen, Rajiv loaned him some stock to start a small shop of his own. He set up his shop in Voi. Voi was a rural shopping centre that served people who were traveling from Mombasa to the hinterland. There were only a few businesses in the small town, most of them run by a few Indians who had settled there after the construction of the railway line. Such shopping centres sprung up along the rail line from Mombasa to Kisumu.

Whenever he faced a situation that required good judgement, V.J. would close his eyes, look up and ask: *What would Rajiv do?* He would then remain silent as he visualized Rajiv facing a similar situation. This was a habit he kept to date.

"That is why I've hung his portrait in the office, in the shops and even at home," V.J. said as he enthusiastically pointed at the golden framed portrait with the inscription: WHAT WOULD RAJIV DO?

John tried to think of any person who had significantly influenced his life; none came to mind. He desired to have such a person, a father who would show him the way, a role model he could be guided and inspired by in his business life, but there just wasn't any. He decided that once he got out of his current predicament he would read biographies of successful entrepreneurs to see if there was one worth adopting as an inspirational father in his life.

"As Rajiv grew old, I wanted to repay him in a big way for taking me in during my lowest point and teaching me business *common sense*. He appreciated my intention but, he told me the only way I could repay him was by sharing his wisdom with at least one hundred people. What a number! They could learn and practice the lessons to transform their failing businesses and make other people's lives better. I needed to create more entrepreneurs who were to be more successful than I."

That was how John's interview had played out in V.J.'s office. But what he needed right now was money, not amazing lessons in business *common sense*. After all, hadn't he read so many great business books which had not helped? Money, not common sense, that's what he needed and urgently. He wanted Michelle and the kids back or he would go crazy!

As a way of concluding their time together, V.J. said, "I was to teach the business *common sense* to one special person." He pointed out that John was that special person. He talked of the signs he'd had to look for to be certain he had met that person. John was perfect match of the description. The only unfortunate thing was that John had very little time to learn all the lessons.

V.J. said, "Son, I have liver cancer." It sounded like it had been rehearsed for a while. It was meant to make John aware of the most important fact of the long conversation. Right there, John realized that V.J. would be more available to him than he may have been to previous protégé entrepreneurs who had learnt from him. This had to be the beginning of something.

CHAPTER 5

THE UNCOMMON COMMON SENSE

SUCCESSPRENEUR SUCCESSPRENEURSHIP APPRENTICE COMMITMENT FORM

I

……………………………………………………………

…………………………………….. commit to the following as I enroll in this programme:

1. I will not quit this program whatever happens;
2. I will attend every session as agreed with my mentor;
3. I will be optimistic even when the end does not seem to come;
4. I will put into action every lesson I learn until it becomes part of me;
5. I will not blame anyone if I do not excel;
6. I will put all the lessons gained into a book.

Signature……………………………………………

…………………..Date……………………………………

The conditions were too easy. John started doubting the seriousness of the whole process, given the simplicity of the rules. Maybe there was a catch. He signed like he had signed all the other school enrolment forms in past years—a mere formality.

Twenty minutes later, V.J. joined him. John handed him the signed card. Without looking at it, he pushed it back to John.

"The hardest commitments to keep are those that we make to ourselves," V.J said. "But I know you will keep them."

John prayed that he would keep them. Many of his friends knew him as the man who kept his word. He honored his promise to others, even when it was too costly. Unfortunately, he rarely made any to himself.

He wondered how he would keep the ones at hand. He thought of laminating the card and carrying it wherever he went, as well as making copies to place next to his bed and his desk, but that felt childish. Maybe it was better to make it his screen saver. He would read them first thing in the morning and last thing at night.

He wanted results. He was committed to this; he had to see it to the end. Only then would he have something to show-off, something to write about. He remembered hearing the words:

> Your role in the program is to offload the wisdom from the depth of my heart and mind. You will record, learn, and practice.

He wondered whether that process was important, but he decided not to ask. And it went on:

> Some of the lessons may contradict what you were taught in school. Others may look trivial, simple or needless. I am a simple man but some of my mentees have been business professors. From the very lessons, they have generated more success for their businesses than from the textbooks. I call it business *common sense.*

John knew this *common sense* was very uncommon. If it was at all common, the thousands of businesses that struggled in spite of being started, owned and ran by brilliant business graduates would be big successes.

"I highly value education and that's why I have given my kids the best that money can buy, but the finest MBAs without business common sense are useless," V.J. said, clarifying his view of education. In the process John learnt a little more about V.J.'s personal life.

V.J. paused as if he was inviting John to meditate on what he had just said. John picked the cue. He was a business graduate, but he had struggled. His cousin, who had barely made it past high school, had built a number of successful businesses. He could count many other successful business people who had minimal education. Maybe too much education was dangerous for entrepreneurship, he thought.

V.J. asked John to write down everything he had learnt from this course. He told John to write down all the questions he had, points for further research and areas of application in his business. The scribble of the faintest pencil is better than the finest memory, V.J. said and John agreed.

John decided to go a step further and use his phone to record all their conversations. On successful completion of the apprenticeship, there was a secret award. Unlike school programs, where the award is known in advance, in this course John would only know the award upon successful completion.

"See you tomorrow, son," V.J. said, bidding him bye as a sign that he had learnt enough for the day. After all, hadn't John come for an interview and not the elaborate *common sense* session he had been subjected to?

Walking away, John wondered: He calls me Son; should I call him Dad?

CHAPTER 6

THE BIRTH OF A SUCCESSPRENEUR

❝Our first session will be about what makes great entrepreneurs. Those who excel in their business ventures, I call them Successpreneur Successpreneurs," V.J. said and John quickly wrote the words on top of the first page in his notebook. He actually wrote: *The Making of a Successpreneur.*

"Are they born or made?" V.J. asked.

"I guess both," John answered.

"Why do you say that?"

"I believe there are people who are born with a Midas touch. The ones who whatever business they lay a hand on to turns to gold. Then there are…"

But before he could continue V.J. raised his hand and John paused. "Like who?" V.J. asked.

John tried to think of a person who has succeeded in all business ventures he got into but he could not recall even a single one. He was certain they were many. All the people he could think of, whose successes cut across all industries, were more of investors than real entrepreneurs. Graciously letting it be, he decided to continue with his dissertation.

"Then there are those who are forced by situations and circumstances to be entrepreneurs." He was not so sure about that part. To avoid further display of ignorance, he ended by saying something inaudible.

"John, all entrepreneurs are born," V.J. said more like a kindhearted teacher correcting a sincerely wrong student. "I said *all!*"

On that note, the debating boy in John was awakened. He had never shied away from an academic debate. But restraining himself from speaking his mind, he decided to remain silent and listen to the reason the old man would say such a dumb thing.

"Everyone is born an entrepreneur. Everyone is born with some ability to solve problems. That is what entrepreneurship is all about—solving problems."

John knew of many people who made money without solving any problem. He gave V.J. examples of the con artists and those who thrived in illegal business. "What about them?" he asked.

"Everyone who earns money legitimately does so by solving problems. Con artists purport to solve problems but in the process defraud their victims. Being a creative crook does not make you an entrepreneur," V.J. said. "The difference should be obvious."

John racked his brain for objection to V.J.'s point, but it was a fruitless search. All the businesses that came to mind seemed to solve a particular problem. He thought about the large supermarket, where he shops when he has money. He goes there because he wants a wide variety of products to choose from. He compared it to his local shopkeeper. He wondered what problem the suburb shop solved. Was it that it provided easy access and the possibility of picking one or two essential groceries in affordable quantities?

"You have no business calling yourself an entrepreneur if your business is not solving any problem. Actually, it will not last for long. If it does, it will not make you much money. What problem does your business solve?" V.J. asked as he suddenly went personal.

"We make websites and consult in internet marketing," John said confidently.

"Are these the problems you solve, John?" V.J. asked, pressing without a hint of mercy.

John felt uncomfortable with this line of conversation. This was the kind of questioning that made him become defensive. Whenever his wife asked such questions he felt under attack. So to say he was irritated right now was an understatement. But he wisely hid his feelings.

When John hesitated to answer, V.J. came to his rescue. "That is your first assignment. I look forward to knowing more about the problems your business solves in the next session."

This man was born before computers and there was no way he could understand the brave new world of internet-driven business. All the same, he had made a commitment to himself to do every assignment and maybe just to please the old man, he would do the assignment. *What would it hurt*, he thought with a shrug.

"While all entrepreneurs are born, successpreneurs are made," V.J. said, rolling on as if nothing had happened. "My desire is to see you become a successpreneur; going beyond the struggle of building a business to creating a successful solution provider, which would be a money machine."

John had a mental vision of the two different characters present there. He saw himself as an entrepreneur and V.J. as a successpreneur. Entrepreneurs were in an ongoing struggle to get a business moving, often facing multiple challenges without knowing the outcome. Their businesses seemed to be caught up in an invisible jail which kept them small and at risk of drowning at the onset of the next storm.

Successpreneurs, on the other hand, were cool, calm and collected. They were purposeful in the way they went about building their businesses. Their livelihood was not dependent on the success of their current venture. Whatever idea they laid their hands on seemed to excel. Resources that they required appeared easily available.

V.J. wanted to teach John how to transition from the former to the latter and John was happy to learn that the raw materials for a successpreneur were nothing more than an entrepreneur who had committed himself to learn and do things according to business *common sense*. That was all it took!

John said, "So how are successpreneurs made?"

"The most important mark of a successpreneur is that they pick the right problems to solve. Just because it is a problem, it is not your problem to solve," V.J. said then paused as John slowly wrote this point.

When John lifted his head to indicate his yearning for more, V.J. continued in his usual calm voice. He said, "Unfortunately, there are people who seek to solve a problem just because they can make some money by doing so. They are there in the *matatu* business just because they see many people standing at bus stops ready to travel. They will jump into farming because they went to the market and could not find certain vegetables. Others will open a shop because a new estate has come up. While all these problems require entrepreneurs to solve them, they are not necessarily good for a successpreneur. A successpreneur chooses *her* problem meticulously."

Her? John wondered about this and asked why V.J. had given successpreneurship a feminine perspective.

"It's because she is a choosy woman. She takes only problems that are tested and qualified through what I refer to as a Wise Choice Criteria," V.J. quipped.

"A Wise Choice Criteria?"

V.J. reached for the phone on the stool, across from the coffee table. "Fix us some coffee, please," he said to the assistant as he went out for his usual smoke.

This must be the cause of his cancer, John thought silently as V.J. exited. Unfortunately, he also knew that stopping to smoke would not heal it. How sad that even bright people sometimes made dumb mistakes. But rather than judge V.J., he felt compassion for him. He feared that V.J.'s smoking had been a habit for years and was hard to break now.

V.J. came back after ten minutes. He felt fired up as he delved into the subject matter of Wise Choice Criteria. John also felt great after a fresh kick from the two cups of Kenyan tea, his addiction.

The Wise Choice Criteria is used consciously, but most of the time unconsciously by successpreneurs to determine which problems to solve. It is after going through this process that they create a business idea. Entrepreneurs start with an idea which they try to make work. Successpreneurs identify a problem then seek to come up with an idea that would solve that problem.

He explained the criteria in detail. He said:

> It is a problem evaluation criteria used only by successpreneurs to determine whether to solve a particular problem or not. For any problem to be right for a successpreneur, it must pass five key tests in the Wise Choice Criteria.

He then added: "Beware of getting into problem-solving that does not engage every part of you. Many successpreneurs are driven by various things—fear of failure, desire to be rich, fear of poverty among others. However, passion for what they do should be top on the list. Whether they are in garbage collection, in pay toilets or in the challenging food business, their passion must be conspicuous. They must have a deep love for what they do.

Passion Test

"If one goes into a business venture without passion, he or she is an opportunist. But there are folks who make a living that way; they are blood thirsty opportunists, not successpreneurs. They don't have a soul," V.J. said biting his lip. It was obvious he couldn't stand them.

John wanted to avoid what he felt was a silly question, but decided to ask anyway. He said, "How do you tell you are passionate about a problem?"

"You can use a passion gauge to measure your passion." V.J. said and opened a document folder to pull out a card. He put it on the table.

After the gauge was set, V.J. looked John in the eye and said, "Son, why are you in your current business?"

"I have a family that needs to be taken care off. I am a trained professional with a five-year work experience. It is what I know how to do."

John recalled the day he collected a cheque of Kshs three million for his employer from the Ministry of Public Works for the website he had developed for them. As far as he could remember, his boss never slept in the office working on that website; he did. Together with his colleague, he'd had the job done. The boss paid them a meager Kshs 100,000.00 each while he pocketed the rest. John felt exploited. He made up his mind to set up a business that would compete with his employer's. The employer knew nothing about web designing.

After he resigned, he felt like he had been rescued from slavery. He suddenly felt free. He was excited. But that excitement lasted only a few months. It was not as rosy as he had envisioned. The only thing that kept him in the business was the hope that one day he would get the big jobs his boss used to get and become a millionaire.

"What can you do if you were not being paid to do it, John?" V.J. asked.

John's greatest joy, in business, had been receiving calls from satisfied clients, who told him their businesses had gotten clients as a result of the website he'd developed for them or the web marketing initiatives he'd executed, leading to improved sales and profits. This was more satisfying than the money they eventually paid for his services—whenever they paid.

V.J.'s face had a fixed smile as he listened to John. John had a happy reminiscence too.

"Short term excitement is not passion," V.J. said. "Many people come up with ideas they are excited about for a brief moment, then the enthusiasm wanes.

That is not passion. A burst of energy when you are trying a new idea or project is not passion. Everybody goes through this stage of excitement when they are starting out on a new business idea."

John had a few friends who thought out a new idea every few months. They were quick to jump onto a new bandwagon. They were always in search of the latest craze in town. In his brief time in Nairobi, he had seen buildings and streets convert from chips and chicken joints, to clothing exhibitions, to roaring pubs and on to restaurants in less than two years. What was so amazing was that many of those businesses were started and run by the same people who had just jumped from yet another short-lived business.

He laughed as he recalled the current craze in the market—quail keeping. *Passion is enduring. If it goes away after a few weeks or months, that is not passion*, he uttered inwardly. *That is not passion,* he repeated. Then, as V.J. looked on in consternation, John verbalized the words with the zeal of a preacher:

THE BUSINESS YOU ARE IN SHOULD BE ALIGNED WITH YOUR PASSION. STARTING AND GROWING A BUSINESS IS TOUGH. THERE ARE MANY UPS AND DOWNS. TO SURVIVE THE DOWNS, YOU REQUIRE A LOT OF PASSION. IT IS PASSION THAT WILL CAUSE YOU TO RISE UP ONE MORE TIME AFTER YOU HAVE

BEEN KNOCKED DOWN. YOU WILL NOT LAST LONG IN A BUSINESS THAT IS NOT ALIGNED WITH YOUR PASSION.

V.J. smiled, then nodded like a sage. John was coming along just fine!

CHAPTER 7

THE MONEY PRINTING BUSINESS

The place was abuzz although most Kenyans were only starting to leave their houses. The restaurant looked like multiple open boardrooms with all the people seemingly in business meetings. There were documents, laptops and tablets everywhere—except on V.J.'s table.

"I help people build their businesses online." That was the way John opened the meeting after they placed their orders. "Most smartphone users search for solutions and service providers on the internet. Businesses are struggling to reach these potential clients. I help them achieve just that."

John proudly explained the problem his business solved, then went on to expound how solving problems is so aligned to his passion and why he is so excited. That brief assignment completely changed how he viewed his business. V.J. looked like a sculptor who had just finished a great art work as he stared at John, whose voice had become more confident and he now held his shoulders high. V.J. thought *How amazing! Nothing major has happened other than the discovery of his passion in his work.* Later, V.J. told him, "Son, did you know that even in daily mundane tasks you can discover your passion? I guess there could be tens of passions that other people too can pick from the problem you are solving," V. J. added, indicating he wanted to move on to other tests.

Opportunity Test

"A problem is only a problem if it hurts so much that people are willing to spend money to solve it. Such a problem is called a business opportunity. Just because a problem exists does not make it an opportunity. Many entrepreneurs create great business solutions and take them to the market only to be bewildered when they discover nobody wants to spend money on that solution. They are shocked when…"

The waiter interrupted them.

"What about creativity?" John asked after the waiter delivered the orders.

"Creativity is great. New ideas are great, but the measure of the greatness of an idea is how it solves a lingering problem or a pressing need of the customers. It may not look very innovative or creative, but if it does, it will put you on the path of becoming a successpreneur," V.J. said as he pulled two cards from his pocket. He seemed obsessed with cards.

He laid one on the table. John recognized the diagram on it. He had learnt about the pyramid. It was Maslow's hierarchy of needs. "I do not know everything about this drawing, but it is a great tool for the Opportunity Test. Every idea must be subjected to a check of the level of problems it solves. One needs to consider the anguish it is to the market. The lower the problem is in the hierarchy, the more likely it is to be a good opportunity because the common problems are more universal and more people find it easy to spend on basic needs than self-actualization needs."

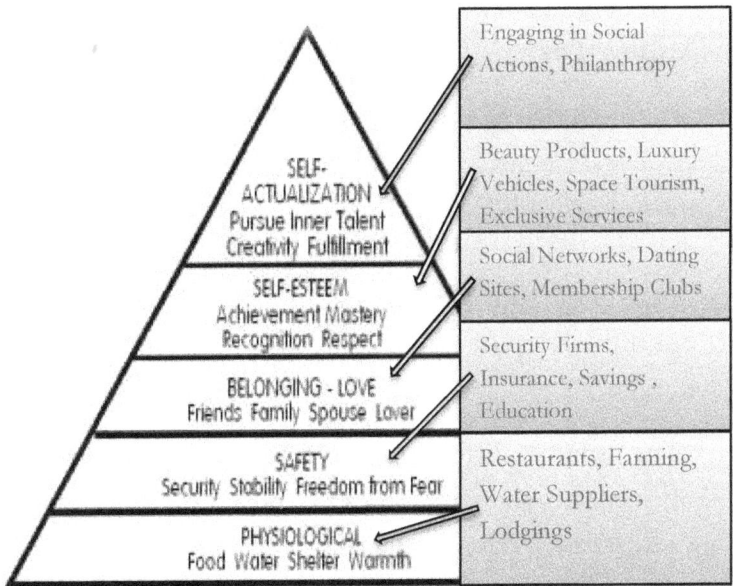

Illustration: Maslow's Hierarchy of Needs: Examples of Business Types Addressing Needs at Different Levels

John wondered how a simple man with a card, with a drawing on it that he did not understand much about, made the card such a great entrepreneurial tool. He had learnt so much about Maslow's hierarchy of needs, but had never applied it anywhere. *Whoever said wisdom is the application of knowledge had V.J. in mind*, John thought.

V.J. said, "This theory of needs has had a lot of criticism in the academic arena, but those who use 1% of an idea are better than those who criticize it 100%, working hard to prove it wrong without ever trying to put it into action.

Money Test

"But, son, that's not all you need to conclude you have an opportunity. It must pass the Money Test. The money test holds that there is a considerable market for your solution. The bigger the number, the better. Beware of solutions that will only interest ten or a hundred people, unless you can make millions from them.

"The point is: different people have different definitions of success when it comes to business. Here is mine: success is a business providing solutions to hundreds of thousands whilst in return making a small profit from every purchase they make. There are others who prefer a large profit from a few customers. The choice is yours. On the other hand, however passionate you are about providing a solution to a problem, if it does not make money, it is not worth being in business—except maybe in the world of *not-for-profit.*"

John was busy taking notes and did not want to interrupt V.J. with trivial questions anymore. V.J. also seemed to talk without a pause. All the same, every word that came from his mouth was well weighed to communicate its intended lesson.

But unable to hold this one, John cleared his throat and said, "Hold on, what about those whose solution is to institutions, organizations and businesses?"

V.J. did not say a word. He just turned the other side of the card and adjusted in the chair. This was what John really wanted. It was what his business was all about, giving solutions to other businesses.

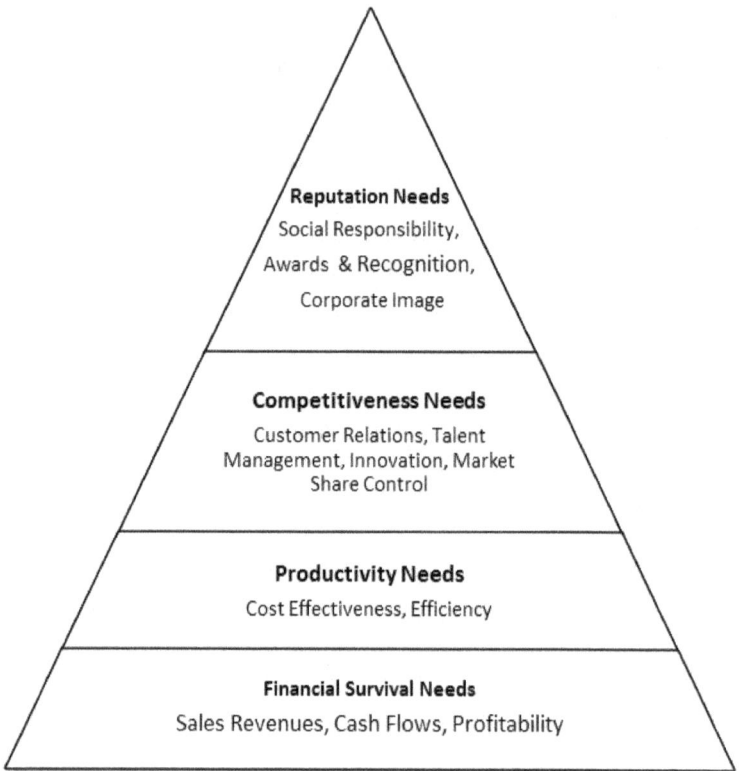

Illustration: Hierarchy of Businesses Needs

John observed that V.J.'s Business Needs Pyramid was similar to Maslow's Hierarchy of Needs Pyramid, but it was focused on the hierarchy of needs of businesses. He also noted that the Business Needs Pyramid also rose from the very basic needs of cash, sales and profits to higher needs such as industry recognition and respect.

Being a bright student helped him understand that this was the most useful tool for him, given that his customers were other businesses. He could see what needs level he needed to address. The same principle applied. The lower the need in the hierarchy, the bigger the market and the more painful it was to the client. This meant one could make a lot more money here, he thought.

Assets Test

"Once your solution passes the passion test, the opportunity test and the money test," V.J. said, "it is time to determine whether you have what it takes to deliver that solution better than anyone else. You evaluate what the required resources are, assess if you have the resources.

"This is the ultimate test of your capacity to provide the solution better than anyone else. If you have the resources that many other people have, you are likely to be getting into a business everyone else will jump into if they see you succeeding. And if there are people with access to superior resources, be sure they will soon render you irrelevant in the market."

John's confidence was deflated. He thought: *Who then can be a successpreneur? Whatever solution one may have, there are people like you, V.J., who would always have vastly more resources than ordinary mortals like me!*

V.J. read John's mind.

"Look, John, I'm not talking about money. It is one of the resources, but probably the least important. I'm also not talking about ownership of resources, I'm talking about access."

V.J. went on to break down the various assets:

- Personal strengths and talents.
- Personal and business connections.
- Professional expertise and special knowledge.
- Personal reputation and brand.
- Financial resources.
- Intellectual property.
- Physical resources.

Noting John's bite of the lip and narrowed eye, V.J. sensed at once that this was an important test and it required further consideration and processing.

Later, after explaining the processing process, V.J. said, "John, not all assets are of equal importance. It all depends on the business idea or solution you want to offer.

There are resources that are critical for your success, there are those that are good to have and those that are not necessary. Knowing the difference for your business idea will make the difference between struggle, failure and success. You should know the difference. If you have all but lack the most critical assets your business is doomed."

And on that note, V.J. finally stood up. He needed to dash to an appointment with his doctor. He handed John another card. John put it in his notebook without checking what was written on it. But as he left, he felt disappointed that the one test he longed for most, the Sweet Spot Test, was not yet covered. He wanted to know what this test really entailed.

Sweet Spot Test

Wisely, once in in the *matatu*, John pulled out the card and there it was. The very definition of Sweet Spot!

> Sweet Spot is that place where your passion, opportunity, money and resources meet.

John suddenly felt ecstatic and pumped a fist in the air as the *matatu* roared into the crowded streets. The diagram he was looking at was simply breathtaking!

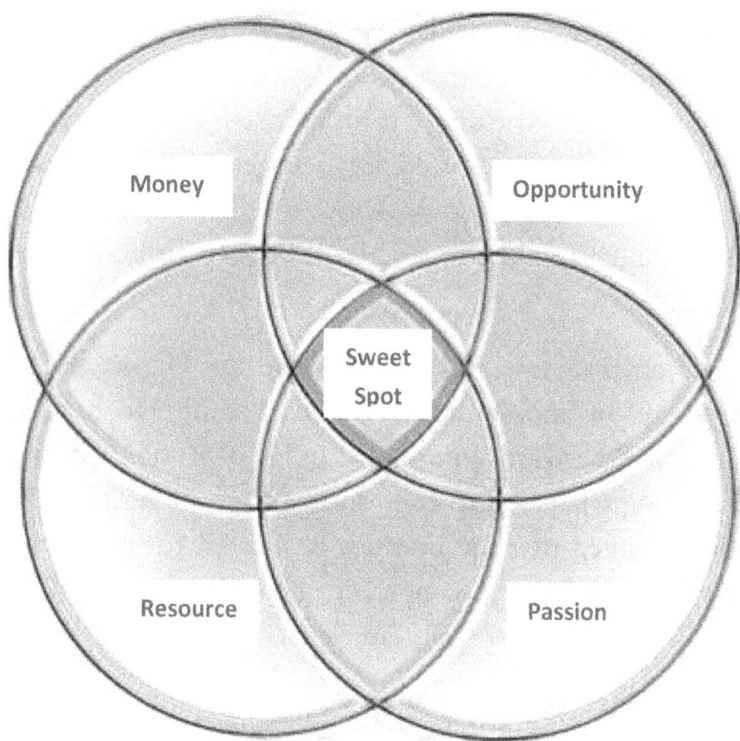

Illustration: Sweet Spot Test

CHAPTER 8

IF YOU ARE GOING THROUGH HELL...

❝Sir, you have a week to go," the office administrator told John as she handed him a final rent demand notice. He'd expected it, but had hoped it would be delayed. He decided not to panic. He believed that help would come from somewhere. The amount owed was Kshs 99,000.00, plus penalties for late payment.

This notice explained why his two employees were not around. They may have heard from the grapevine of its imminent delivery. They decided to leave the premises to avoid embarrassment.

But he was wrong. The two guys never feared any embarrassment. They wanted money. After giving up on ever being paid their dues, they'd decided to take the two laptops before anyone could restrain them. One of the conditions of the notice was that he was not allowed to take any asset from the office. They got wind of it and acted. They beat him to the game.

He had been paying them in bits and pieces. Their salaries were now in three months arrears. Maybe he should have fired them the first time he'd experienced financial difficulties, but he never did. Since he'd delayed, they became too casual on the job. They felt no obligation to give their best. They spent a lot of time on the fast internet, waiting for the end of the month.

Do not sweat the small stuff, one of his favourite books advised. But this was not small stuff. This was real and scary stuff. He felt like a trapped gazelle waiting for the hunter to come for the kill. He prayed for a sudden miracle of financial provision because he knew that all the lessons he had learnt from V.J. were great, but could not help him out of his present predicament.

Indeed, John was not lazy. He had not refused to pay anyone his dues. He had anticipated that his customers would keep their payment promises, which they didn't do. Every day, he had hoped one would call him for a cheque, but none had so far.

He looked at the other start-up entrepreneurs located in the shared office space and wondered whether they had ever been through this experience. He longed to be an employee.

As an employee, when things got bad, one could just walk out and look for another job. As an entrepreneur, however, he was too attached to this business baby he had pampered for five years now. The problem was that the baby had refused to grow. He behaved like a one year old, 100% dependent on him.

When you find yourself in a hole, you should stop digging, is common advice. John was in a deep hole and remaining in business was sinking him deeper into a bottomless pit of debt. Time to shut it down, he'd finally made up his mind. He planned to silently disappear from the city and spend some time in the village. That would allow him time to heal. Trouble was that he was too attached to what he had poured the whole of himself into for five long years.

"We will bring the laptops once our salaries are banked," the senior of his two employees texted him after his persistent calls.

His employees had done exactly what he had done to his last employer. He had sent his resignation email on a Saturday evening. He did not pick his boss' calls for a couple of days. Now he would not advice anyone to behave similarly as this was tantamount to burning bridges one may need later in life.

His former boss was forgiving and they mended their relationship. They even went further to collaborate on a few projects, with John seeking his advice on various business issues. At the height of their work, the man once told John to accept that problems and business are inseparable. But by far the best advice he gave John was that when things went wrong they were giving him feedback. They were telling him something!

"Listen carefully, get the message and act quickly before it is too late," he told John. That advice had sounded hollow one year ago, but he felt he should try it now.

As he sat at his desk, he decided to listen to the messages. He heard nothing.

He logged on his Facebook page. Maybe it would offer some helpful distraction. He had posted a question earlier in the week, asking for inspirational quotes for a struggling entrepreneur. The response was massive. But the one that impressed him was:

> "If you are going through hell, don't stop." — Sir Winston Churchill

His mind shifted to V.J.'s predicament. How come V.J. did not appear so fearful of his situation? *Suppose I was the one who had been diagnosed with cancer? Which was worse? Cancer or money problems?*

Because of developments at the office, John decided he required at least a break from the sessions. He would be candid with V.J. about his dire situation. V.J. was a reasonable man who would listen to him. He would understand that at this point what John needed was not lessons, but money.

During the break he would focus on getting that money. He was not breaking his commitment; this was an act out of necessity. *I am just doing what any man in my situation would do*, he told himself.

John later went to the offices of the National Youth Enterprise Fund. There, he ran into the kind rebuke of a receptionist who said, "You educated people do not come for this money. It is your money!"

He didn't know what to tell her. He had decided not to lie down but fight on. A friend had advised him to check with the Fund. It was a good option for youthful entrepreneurs. He was one. He was not great, but he was good enough for the money. If he got the cash, he would do a different kind of business. Maybe he would run a shop. Shops guarantee cash flow. That was what he wanted. Big profits were wonderful, but at this point what he wanted was cash, not profit.

The lady came back smiling. He anticipated great news from whoever she had gone to consult in the back office. She said, "Sir, you are a few days older than the maximum eligible age." He could not be disappointed any further!

The lady said, "I don't know how to help you. You are not a woman!"

John could tell that those words were her attempt at sounding supportive. He did not need that. He walked out. He had forgotten he had just turned thirty six. In Kenya, one was considered a youth up to thirty five.

He was no longer a youth!

He then thought of this: The worst lies we tell are the ones we tell ourselves. He had heard those words many years back, but had always considered those lies to be optimism. Today, though, he needed a big dose of truth. He went to the nearby Nairobi Central Chapel.

He sat on the bench closest to the altar. He sat there silently. The biblical statement, *truth will set you free*, played in his troubled mind. It may not have been a business mantra, but it applied to his current business situation. He confessed his many sins. He petitioned God to stop punishing him and even admitted his inability to solve his problems.

John was slowly becoming truthful with himself. A new John was emerging. But then he slept. He later woke up feeling rested. His mind was at peace. As he looked at his phone, though, he saw a message flash. *They have kidnapped me*, it read. He called back!

———

Shalom Hospital was one of the largest private hospitals in the country. It prided itself as the best in cancer treatment in the region. When John's mother had battled the disease, he had visited the cancer care clinic. It was heart-rending for the family when they could not raise the required treatment fee. The cancer tests alone were more expensive than the air ticket to India, where they were warned she would need to go if she was to pull through. Later, heeding that warning, they opted to fundraise to send their mother to a hospital in Mumbai for surgery and chemoradio treatment. Unfortunately, the malignant disease had spread to other organs. She passed on a few months after.

He asked a lady cleaner for directions to the VIP Wing. The lady courteously accompanied him there. John was impressed by that level of customer service. He wished all hospitals handled relatives and friends of in-patients the same way. It was not a bad place to be held hostage in, but only if you were in good health.

V.J. was in high spirits. John wondered why the doctor who'd diagnosed him thought he needed emergency rest as further tests were conducted. John wondered whether this was finally the right time to call off the commitment.

But right then V.J. said, "Son, have you gained anything so far from our talks and exercises?"

"They have been valuable. I have learnt a lot and gained a lot of business lessons. I'm indeed grateful for the opportunity." John hoped V.J. would catch the hint by using the past tense. "It has been a pleasure, sir!"

"Wait, son, you don't sound or look okay, what's the matter?" V.J. asked thoughtfully.

It was unusual, in the business world, for people to be interested in the personal matters of others. People were rarely human beings. They were tools, resources or means to an end. People were employees, service providers, suppliers or customers. They mattered for the results they produced. John had accepted this as the world he was operating in. Sadly, at this point he was a broken human being who needed someone to take interest in him as such—someone who would not mind him pouring his troubles and understand them at a business owner's level. All his friends had stable jobs. They would not comprehend his current predicament.

Exhaling in a staggered fashion, he said, "Sir, I hate to bother you when you are on this bed, but the bottom has dropped off. I'm quitting this business thing. I'm not made for it."

V.J. listened. His whole being was present. That encouraged John to say all he wanted to say. He felt he mattered to this man. The old man had drawn some circles on one of the prescription notes. He wrote a few things on it as John spoke.

Finally V.J. said, "You know what? That sounds like the life of a successpreneur who is about to strike it big in business. It is always darkest before dawn!

"Let's take my example. There were times I felt like I was all alone against the world. I felt lost. But those experiences later became useful to me in business.

"I have learnt to be patient in those situations. I have learnt to have inner peace regardless of the storms around me. I have learnt to detach myself from the situation and observe it from a distance so as to get a better view of it. But most importantly, I have learnt how to solve the problems I can and accept the ones that I cannot."

John's tears formed, but V.J. acted like he didn't see them. He asked John to fix drinks for both of them, then he said: **Whatever problem we face, it gives us an opportunity to either deal with it or allow it make us victims.** He asked John to draw closer as he laid on the bed the paper he was scribbling notes on.

John looked at it and all he saw was his problems written around a small circle.

"Inside that circle is John's power," V.J. said. "Outside that circle are all the problems you have talked about. The more you focus on those problems, the smaller is your power circle. You become a victim. The more you focus on the power you have to seek solutions to your problems, the bigger the circle and the more the power you have over the problems."

John considered what the sage had just said. The sage was right. John had focused so much on his problems to the point he felt like a small insect. But wasn't he justified in his suffering? Maybe he was, and maybe it even felt good to be soothed with loving, caring words, but what V.J. wanted was for him to focus on finding a solution to his problems, not seeking sympathy.

The most potent words inside the circle were: *what am I going to do to solve it?* That question was like a command to a highly powerful computer. It ordered the mind to start looking for solutions.

Inside the circle he wrote the answers he got.

V.J. finally fell asleep as John created more circles in his notebook. He loved the game.

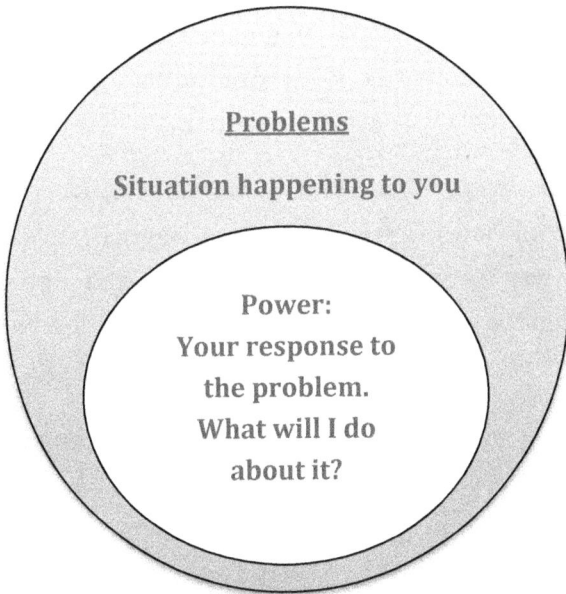

Illustration: Power Circle

———

Tim provided start-up entrepreneurs with a good place to run their businesses. The location provided a great office address, a classy meeting room, a working desk with high speed internet and secretarial services. It saved one major costs that come with running and owning an office.

Although Tim visited the place often, he rarely spoke to his clients. He had a desk reserved for him, but rarely used it. When he had an issue with any tenant, he avoided confrontation. All he did was to write a short memo that was placed on the tenant's desk by the office assistant. If the matter went out of hand, policemen became handy. It was a simple as that.

John had become solution-oriented. V.J.'s problem solving tool had inspired him. One way to be solution oriented was to talk to people you you'd had a problem or differences with. That was why he had come back to Tim's this morning.

As soon as he got in and saw a chance to engage, he told Tim to look at the matter differently. He said, "If you kick me out at this point, you will lose the money I owe you. I will not have a place to complete my clients' projects and I will not get paid. If you allow me one more month, however, I will pay at least 30% of what I owe you and in three months I will have cleared all the outstanding debt. My tenancy agreement will be up-to-date. What do you say?"

After a short silence, Tim accepted the offer and asked John to put it in writing and give it to the office assistant.

As John wrote the commitment, he whispered to himself that V.J. was so right. It had worked. He felt powerful as he went back to his desk.

He scribbled the names of all the customers who owed him money. He decided to call the actual debtors personally to make payments. He had been busy calling either the accountants or the people who wrote cheques, which hadn't worked. He had rarely spoken to the real debtors, who could get him paid. He was scared to talk to them and did not consider it 'good business manners' to talk to them.

Two hours later, he felt like he owned the world. He was surprised that some of the decision makers were not aware he had not been paid. Others had minor issues that were easy to finalize so that he got paid. Two or three did not mind to make payment for the partial work he'd done. But there were others who were not in the office. He promised he would keep calling till he was able to get a hold of them. After the calls, he had pledges amounting to Kshs 300,000.00, to be paid in three weeks. The bosses also consented to follow-up on agreed timelines.

Just as Tim had asked him to put his vow in writing, he sent e-mails to all the people he had called, summarizing the discussions they had had. He felt like these were promises he had made rather than the clients. He could finally afford a cup of tea and *chapati* in the cafeteria downstairs. But he felt he had two more calls to make.

"Bring it on!"

He was all alone in the lift and started visualizing himself facing Michelle and resolving all the issues he had spent too much time talking about with his boys. He even recalled that a while back he had tried to call Maina, on Classic FM, to vent about his inconsiderate wife, but his call had not gone through because there had been too many people making similar calls.

Looking back now, he was glad the call had flopped. If he'd had a problem with his wife, it was only with her he could get a solution, not by venting over the air for Kenyans to know he was a man. In fact, didn't doing something like that make him…not man enough? Once more, he thought of V.J.'s words and for the first time felt he was dealing with a sage for sure!

CHAPTER 9

THE BLOOD OF BUSINESS

❝It is the size of a child's fist. It requires immediate surgery," V.J. said as he squeezed John's hand with a smile that covered fear.

John knew that a tumor as big as what V.J. had just demonstrated required swift action. And being a recurrence didn't help matters. Four years ago, V.J. had had another tumor removed. He was fortunate that it had been picked up early. Today, although V.J. was strong, he did not seem very optimistic. And neither did he look forward to chemotherapy.

A knock interrupted the silent moments the sage and the young man were sharing, which were marked by hisses of pain and shedding of tears. A middle aged couple walked in. V.J. managed to get up and gave each a warm hug. John could tell they were more than just friends. Anne and Oscar Mibinda were household name in business circles in the nation.

Born into poor families, the two had managed to see themselves through college by handling odd jobs and encouraging each other whenever the going was tough. After they got married, they tried a couple of businesses, but they all faltered, causing them to wonder what magic billionaires used to amass so much wealth.

They finally had a breakthrough when Oscar met V.J.

"How would you like having siblings?" V.J. asked John after hearty exchanges with the couple.

The question lingered in John's mind. He was not sure to whom it had been directed. It was never answered. The easy talk between V.J. and the couple went on. John was a silent listener. He picked bits and pieces of V.J.'s well-kept private life in the process.

V.J. got married in his late forties. The couple was blessed with two children, a boy and a girl. However, the marriage did not last long. After the divorce, V.J.'s wife left the country and remarried in Europe. The kids had troubled lives. V.J.'s son later died of cocaine overdose while the girl joined her mother.

V.J. maintained contact with the girl for a while, but she passed on due to breast cancer, leaving behind two children, who were being taken care of by their father.

V.J. wished he had been more available to his family, but that had not happened and there was nothing he could do about it now. John felt sorry for him.

"They say I need to travel to Delhi tomorrow for the surgery," V.J. said. His voice was grim.

John was stunned. *Travel tomorrow?* He knew immediate treatment was important, but it also meant an end to the programme. *What lousy timing is this? Just when I was starting to experience positive results?* At the rate things had played out, John had been hopeful of getting his wife back in less than a month, but with this break it was going to be much longer if ever. He moaned inwardly as he painfully wore back his pessimistic goggles.

V.J. closed his eyes as pain crept through every part of his body. Anne pressed the bell. A nurse came and administered a painkiller. The visitors were then asked to allow him to rest.

But before they walked out, V.J. looked his son in the eye and said, "Oscar, please continue with John from where we had reached. He is your younger brother. Once my body allows it I will be back to celebrate his graduation." He smiled. "I know it won't be long!"

It was a deeply emotional moment for John. His cheeks got wet with tears. Then as the couple left the room, V.J. signaled John and asked the doctor to excuse them briefly. He pulled out an envelope from a book on the bedside desk.

Taking John's hand, V.J. said, "Son, it is better to owe one person than to owe too many people. You should never pay your debts to the extent that you cannot live.

You need to eat and your family needs to eat as well. If you and your family are hungry you will be unproductive. Once you leave this place, do the math of all you owe and all you require to live on for the next three months. Write the amount to yourself. It is signed. My accountant will expect a cheque from you of the same amount ninety days from today."

It was confusing, but he finally got it. As he walked out, he avoided looking back. His eyes were filled with tears.

———

Cash is the blood of any business. Without cash, there is doom and gloom. Now John had enough to pay off his debts. And thinking about it, he recalled what a financial coach once told him. *Pay your debts with a sense of gratitude.* Of course he had wanted to all along, but had never gotten that opportunity. There were always more bills than the money. Today he was going to put into practice that advice.

The experience of struggling financially had taught him some successpreneurship money lessons and he was going to list them as soon as he got back to the office. The four leading ones were:

- Do not incur any expense unless it is necessary for your business.

- Adjust your lifestyle.
- Do not make plans based on others' promises.
- Customers pay when they pay, not when they say they will pay.

John was told these were the four lessons that had enabled eBiz to survive the five hard years they found themselves in the doldrums. He was going to use them to survive now and in the future.

CHAPTER 10

IT IS NOT HOW GOOD AN IDEA IS

O scar had a taste for fine things. The office design and its fittings, the furniture, the wall posters and everything in the office oozed class. The bronze-framed wall hangings, with photos of Henry Ford, an African Lion hunting and the giant mustard tree spoke of the source of his inspiration.

Cool classical music spelt further that this was a man who had polished taste. To make it even better, a guitar hung on one corner of the office. John enjoyed being in this office. One wall of the office was a solid library, with books covering diverse fields. At exactly 8:15 a.m., Oscar arrived. The purpose of this meeting was for the two protégés of V.J. to get acquainted with each other on a deeper level. They shared how they met V.J. and the difference he had made in their lives. They also talked about their business journeys. Although both had been through V.J.'s lessons, Oscar had achieved the greatness that John now aspired for. John felt an even greater sense of assurance that taking V.J.'s offer had been a great decision. Oscar was the proof! John learnt that V.J. had made a contingency to hand him over to Oscar in case his health had deteriorated.

But it had happened too soon. V.J.'s health had deteriorated so fast that there was no clear handover. The two men now agreed to proceed. There was neither set curriculum nor a fixed process this great program followed. V.J. had always taken his students from the point they were at, in their entrepreneurship journey, and hardly were any two students at the same level of understanding, experience and business exposure. V.J. had known, after meeting John, that Oscar was a close match to the new son in certain aspects.

Oscar decided to take John through the process the same way V.J. had once taken him. He had not done it before, but from his success, he was confident he would do it with John. He now had a chance to help someone achieve greatness, which should have been a solemn goal for everyone who achieved success.

Oscar committed himself to share the two lessons that had made the biggest difference in his business. That was what they were to focus on in the next meeting. Before then, he gave John a preparation assignment.

——

Shoppers Central was the largest supermarket chain in the country. It served millions of customers every year across the Eastern Africa Region. V.J. built it from scratch, after he came back to Kenya from Uganda;

after Idi Amin took over power and expelled all the Indians from that landlocked East African nation. The first store was opened in Kisumu.

John walked through the shop's floors, trying to discover anything unusual about how the business was run. He had done this in the last four days, visiting various other competing stores. After three hours of comparative shopping, all he saw, that was superior in *Shoppers Central,* was a more orderly arrangement of shelves, wider isles that allowed easy movement in the shop, enjoyable background music, helpful attendants and happy customers. He had visited all listed supermarkets, as per Oscar's assignment. His task was to figure out how *Shoppers Central* was different from its competition, particularly on how it made money.

He called Oscar and said, "I cannot see anything that makes it different. Please give me a clue!"

"Talk to Sylvia, the branch manager," Oscar advised.

The following day, at 10.00 a.m., John met Sylvia. He asked the big question: how is *Shoppers Central* different from other supermarket chains?

Given John's relationship with V.J., whose large portrait looked back at visitors in all the offices, Sylvia was open and let him in on a lot of information.

"Our most important business asset is our customers. People wrongly think we sell products. No. We have created millions of happy and loyal customers. Over 90% of our customers shop twice in our shops every month. They spend about Kshs 20,000.00 every two months. We make it easier for them to want to come often and spend as much as possible. Whenever one visits, regardless of whether they buy or not, we give them a great shopping experience."

John had always shopped here. He had always come back. He had thought he made the decision to come back on his own. Now it was clear that there was a strategy to make him come again and again. It stunned him!

Sylvia said, "These loyal customers are what *Shoppers Central* sells to manufacturers, importers and resellers of the products customers buy. They pay to get a share of these customers' shopping budget. They are charged a fee to stock their products, depending on the shelf space they occupy. Unlike other supermarkets, *Shoppers Central* does not own a single item in our stores. We are not in the business of buying and selling products at a profit.

In other words, the guarantee distributors get from *Shoppers Central* is that they will sell more of their goods at better margins than they would ever sell at any other store. That is the secret."

John couldn't believe it. "Are you serious?"

"We don't have suppliers and we don't own any stock, but we have some of the largest warehouses," Sylvia said. "The vendors deliver their products to us and we distribute those products to the various stores as they are required.

"We have world class inventory management systems which allow us to manage their stocks better than they would. We advise and train their staff on excellence in displaying and selling their products as well as serving customers. For any entity to be allowed to trade with us, its customer service has to meet our standards."

And on that note, John was finally ready for Oscar's session. He was doing this for Michelle and the kids!

———

Oscar showed John around the vast MDG Industrial Complex. Oscar's first business had involved selling milk. It went by the name Maziwa Distributors. The business had failed utterly. He then met V.J. and after much thought, he came up with MDG, an acronym of Maziwa Distribution Group.

The complex was throbbing with, activities in different factories and warehouses. It left John confused as to whether this was one or multiple firms. He also wondered how Oscar kept track of all the activities that appeared to run on a roller coaster.

He counted fifteen different product brands. Each brand had at least four product lines. The workers at the conveyor belts stood at one point, repeating a single task for hours on end. It was a perfected art. Employees blended in with machinery in a unified effort that involved minimal talking. Everyone knew what they were supposed to do to maintain orderliness. The sounds made by the machines were monotonous. John thought he could not survive a day here. He was not a routine guy. He loved spontaneity and continuous change. The conveyor belt did not allow for that. He knew, deep down, that he would have loved to own and operate a small manufacturing plant, but for now that had to remain a future thing. Oscar was ready for him.

———

"How do we make money?" Oscar asked.

John felt he knew the answer because he had just seen impressive manufacturing going on. It should have been obvious to anyone, who cared to look, that the giant MDG manufactured and distributed consumer goods at a decent profit. Why else would they have production machines? Why would they need so many hands?

But John did not respond.

Noting John's calculated silence, Oscar cleared his throat and started to talk. Unlike V.J., who did a lot of telling, Oscar taught more by showing. John enjoyed this method better. It required less thinking. Oscar went ahead to answer his own question, the one he'd just asked John, by explaining his business.

He said, "For example, John, the *Eagle Soap* line you saw is not our product. We manufacture and distribute it on behalf of someone else. They pay us to do it. *Soft Baby* too is an international brand that we package for the local market. The product is imported when it is 80% complete. The formula is secret.

"*Smile Dental Care* products are our brands that are manufactured and packaged in Egypt on our behalf. In Kenya we only do their marketing and distribution. In other words, we manufacture and package products on behalf of our competitors and some do the same for us. All those are different models for our business.

"By the way, most entrepreneurs do not understand the concept of business models. As a result, there are numerous copycats. Unfortunately, they struggle since they do not understand the model behind the success.

Some models such as buying at low price and selling at a higher profit are easy to copy, while others are not as obvious. Whenever you see a successful business, seek to interrogate and understand the model it is built on. You become a wise successpreneur that way."

"So why don't you use one business model for all your products?" John asked. He was always at ease with difficult subjects. He had always been top of his class in school. However, this models subject seemed too hard to grasp. Maybe this was the big secret successpreneurs did not share with other entrepreneurs.

Oscar said, "To get maximum value from a business opportunity, you need the right idea and the right business model." He went into detail, explaining that a model was the execution strategy for a business idea. As he talked, the concept became clear to John. John wrote different definitions in his note book. The notebook had now become a must-carry everywhere. He wrote this:

    a. A business model explains how a business is designed to make money.

    b. A business model is the strategy for executing one's business idea.

    c. A business model is the architectural design of a business.

The later, from Oscar's explanation, he wrote:

> The right business model is one that will give your customers the best solution at the lowest affordable price while enabling you to make the highest possible profits with the resources you have.

He noted that the satisfaction customers needed came before making money.

> The reason we don't use the same model for all our product is because of the uniqueness of each target customer segment, their unique problems, available resources and acceptable profit margins. A uniform model would have been disastrous for our business.

As he wrote the words Oscar was sharing, he couldn't help but hear V.J.'s voice. V.J. had said it was not great ideas that made great businesses. That the right model, one that was well designed and executed, did. That the model chosen set an entrepreneur, a successpreneur and a job holder a part.

John hoped he would one day teach a struggling entrepreneur this game changer. Satisfied with the quality of notes he had taken so far, he asked, "How do I create the right business model for my idea? "Asking the right questions made him feel intelligent. He needed to build this into a habit, he thought, that way he would always stand out! But Oscar needed to attend a meeting. Before he stepped out, he pulled out a card from his desk. It was fancier than the ones V.J. had been using. "Go through this, John. When we meet on Friday we will use it to answer your question."

On that note, the meeting ended and John set the card on his lap. He needed to study it right away for fear of competing interests getting in the way later.

3. **Value Delivery** – what infrastructures and logistical arrangements that you will use to get the customer access the value			
1. Value Offering - Pain killer, pleasure enhancing physical product service that customer will buy	**6. Critical Assets/Resources** – networks, finances, expertise, licenses, people you require to develop the value and deliver it to the customer	**5. Critical Activities** – all the operations that need to work for the business to create and deliver the value to the customer	**2. Target Customer** People who: i) Pay for the product ii) Use the product iii) Influence buying decisions for the product
	8. Profit The difference between money actually paid by the customer and all the costs incurred in creating and delivering the value		
	4. Marketing – How will you make customers aware of your product, get them to make first purchase and keep them coming back again		
7. Revenues Model: How customers will pay to get value e.g. rent, subscription, licenses, lease buy the product pay for the service.			
9. Growth Model: How do you foresee the business growing to reach more customers, increase revenues and grow profits.			

Illustration: Summary of Business Model Building Blocks

CHAPTER 11

MONEY HAS NO SOUL, SO THE MODEL

John woke up to a sunny day and looked forward to another session with Oscar. As he prepared, he recalled words he'd read in a business journal:

> Be in love with your business idea, but never emotionally attached to a business model. The idea is you destination, the model is the means. If your destination is Mumbai, you could choose to travel by road, air or sea. The destination can be sentimental. The choice of means is a cold practical. Regrettably, many entrepreneurs are emotionally attached to the model.

But the fact that lingered and caused him to marvel since then was this:

Money has no soul.

He thought the same applied to a business model. It too was soulless! An hour after waking up and preparing, John stood silently next to Oscar in the lift, headed to the ground floor restaurant for breakfast.

After placing their orders Oscar didn't waste time—he delved into the business model elements.

Marriage Between Value And Target Customers

"Listen, the business value is the painkiller or pleasure enhancing aspect of your product, your service or a combination of both. It is what you call a product. The product should be designed to kill some pain or create some pleasure for the customer. How you plan to design this product is critical to your business model.

"Take for instance MDG's toothpaste products. If the value we want to offer is teeth whitening, how should we create it? Manufacture our own product? Import a proven product? Get a manufacturing licence? A model should answer all these questions," he said.

Then just as quickly he asked, "So what value does *Shoppers Central* give?"

John could tell this was a question-laden session. He was glad Oscar kept them rhetorical, though, because he didn't have answers to them even though he found them engaging and pointed. They crystallized ideas and had to be a key requirement for successpreneurship, he thought. *Now tell me the answer!* His eyes were on Oscar.

Target Customers

Oscar said, "John, the point is this—having great value or a product is not sufficient. Your target customer for a product must be clearly defined." He gave examples of businesses that had failed because they had great products channeled to the wrong customers. John could also remember a few of such organizations.

"In determining the best customer for your value," Oscar said, "consider the population and segment it based on, and the type of pains they could be having. Assuming your value is toothpaste, the population must be made up of people who have teeth. But listen to this, John, because it is critical: such a population also has diverse segments that have different pains. Would you want to list them?"

Oscar started to devour his breakfast as John went through the various segments.

People who:

- brush as a habit;
- are conscious of good breath;
- have stained teeth;
- have dental diseases;
- suffer from sensitive teeth;
- cannot afford toothpaste;
- do not like the taste of existing toothpaste;
- have kids who hate brushing their teeth.

"Great," Oscar said impressed. "So which is the right segment for you?"

John mumbled and trailed off.

Oscar came to his rescue. "If you are starting out, pick a segment that has had an ignored need by the existing players."

That simple? John wondered why it had not been so obvious to him. *I should have known that!*

Oscar said, "In many cases, but not always, that niche is too small for the 'big boys' but big enough for a starter. A case in point, if there are toothpaste consumers who take fruit juice, chew gum or take flavoured beverages to get rid of toothpaste aftertaste, it may indicate there is a segment of the market that is already trying to get a product that leaves a fruity taste after brushing. You could pick it if your toothpaste can achieve that."

John wondered whether that was the next toothpaste product from MDG. Oscar, reading his mind, confirmed that a new line of fruit flavoured toothpaste products were to be launched in a couple of days. They were available in orange, mango and apple flavours.

He added, "Value creation and choice of the target market segment are intertwined. A mismatch calls for adjustment of either to achieve a workable alignment. Alternatively, you could rethink your value or the segment."

From that point on, Oscar went into finer detail about how the value of *Shoppers Central* was aligned to the Middle and Upper Class customer segments.

John thought of his eBiz Services and it dawned on him that he did not have any clear value. He had not even thought of which market segment was right for his services.

He was a real hustler. He just woke up and aimed for whoever came his way and he addressed their needs. If he thought he had been focused, now he knew he needed to focus even better.

Value Delivery Channel

Oscar interrupted his flow of thought by saying, "John, the method you choose for delivering the value to the customer will enhance or dilute that value. And that is the third element—the delivery channel."

John noticed the repetition. It was probably intended to emphasize the importance of what was said.

"Had V.J. wanted to offer the lowest priced products to customers, his shopping chain would have been the worst channel to do so. His stores are very expensive to rent, design and manage. They are ideal to deliver the shopping experience that the upper-middle and upper class desire and are willing to pay for."

John wrote:

> The value you want to deliver and the customer
> you are targeting will determine what value
> delivery channel to use. A wrong channel will
> dilute value and consequently be unattractive to
> the customer.

Marketing

When Oscar moved to the fourth element, marketing,
John was excited. He liked marketing and considered
himself an expert. It was his subject of choice at the
university in spite of all its demerits. And to make the
choice an even more daring move, there were few
marketing jobs at that time.

Defying the odds and sticking in marketing, John had
once read that Peter Drucker, the father of modern
management, had considered marketing the highest of
business endeavours, coupled with innovation. He had
lamented that:

> When the economy is struggling, many business
> people and managers consider marketing a
> luxury. They cut on marketing related costs.
> Unfortunately, it is in such times that marketing
> is most critical. When the economy is in an
> upswing, much of marketing activities become
> wasteful. Marketing is an investment. Well

> planned and executed marketing gives better returns than any other form of business investment.

"What are you thinking of?" Oscar asked, looking John in the eye. "Rather, let me ask this: what is marketing?"

John said, "Before you say anything about marketing, let me give you a definition."

"You're sure?"

"Try this," John said and cleared his throat.

"I'm ready!"

John said:

> Marketing is about getting customers to know about your value, make the first purchase, then keep coming back as often as possible for more of the product for as long as they are alive.

Oscar made a face like *really?*

John saw the face and said, "Look, Oscar, professors and business schools try to understand what is going on in the real world and make it fit into some concepts like 4Ps, 7Ps or whatever other Ps and Qs. For us in the trenches, we don't care what you call it. We just do what we have to do. We try to get people to buy a lot of our product as often as possible for as long as they are breathing. Everything we do is marketing. That, to me, is the successpreneur's marketing philosophy."

Oscar noted John's serious tone and his sudden fire and decided to let him talk on.

"Those in the trenches apply the principles of the trenches, being *street smart*, not the ones in textbooks. What I need is to rid my mind of textbook material to create room for street wisdom!" he said.

Oscar smiled, surprised by John's sudden burst of energy. Adjusting in his chair, he said, "John, are you okay? Would that be a smart thing to do?"

"Of course it would be," John deadpanned. "There are many business graduates struggling to run businesses while guys like V.J., who have no more than basic schooling, create successful business ventures every day. The difference is the business wisdom learnt from the trenches. That is what all entrepreneurs need!

"One day, after becoming a successpreneur for a while, I will have a course titled Masters in Business Wisdom. It will focus on lessons from the real world of starting and growing a business to great heights of success."

Oscar drew a deep breath and was about to say something, but changed his mind and let it be. Getting up, he said, "Let's take a break, John!"

CHAPTER 12

SKINNING THE MODEL FURTHER

During the break, John sensed that his fire was back. Rather than go to the bathroom or have a chat with folks around, he sat at a corner and pulled out a book he last read a year ago. In it, he focused on a complicated paragraph that he had to translate into something he could understand. It was essentially this:

> The greatest determinant of success in any aspect of life is always the most boring, the most tedious and is always the one that requires extraordinary commitment to master. That is why there are always a few people at the top. They have mastered how to achieve success while the rest of the crowd pushes and pulls at the base.

What that meant, John thought, was that to get to the top, one had to put in long hours of learning, hard work and mastery. One had to practice and persevere even when one failed until success was achieved.

He realized there were times one would be alone and lonely trying to create what only he or she could understand, but he wasn't going to be daunted by that. *I may have to sacrifice fun and focus on that one thing that no one else is interested in for me to succeed,* he thought silently as the book's message took hold. He recalled what he had learnt about the 10,000 Hours Rule and the discipline of Pay Now and Play Later.

It came down to this:

Successpreneurs spend long hours creating and building businesses that offer great value to customers and in return make a lot of money. They understand business models. Said in the jargon familiar only to initiated business minds, this simple concept sounded hefty, but that's what it was—working hard!

Oscar swept in and found him at the corner. He quickly shut the book and walked back to the session table. Now settled, Oscar said, "Seems like you had a fun break with a book. I didn't know you were such a reader. John smiled and said he was one when occasion called for it.

"That's great. Let's get going again, shall we? The fourth block focuses on the key activities it takes for a business model to deliver results. While planning the model, one needs to consider all the activities to engage in to create the value, communicate it to the customer, deliver it, and get paid for it."

Oscar gave the example of the milk business that had failed before he met V.J. to illustrate this point further.

Oscar listed the key activities. John learnt the A-Z of producing a simple packet of milk and nodded as Oscar listed them. The list looked like this:

- Varied licences for carrying out the business
- Meeting farmers to persuade them to make him their preferred milk buyer and organize milk collection schedule
- Assess the quality of the milk delivered
- Make transportation arrangements of the perishable produce
- Processing and packaging of the product
- Delivery to shopkeepers
- Marketing processed milk to shopkeepers
- Handling excess stock and unsold stock
- Storage of the milk not sold
- Handling of spoilt milk and other complaints
- Money collection and banking

Oscar shifted in the chair as he always did when he judged that what he was about to say was critical. He then said, "I never thought much of these activities until I was already in the business, yet each of these activities had a hidden risk for me: dishonest farmers who added water into the milk, untrustworthy salesmen, bad debt shopkeepers, spoilt milk, unhappy customers, etc. Each day, at least one of these activities went wrong and the business suffered. I lost money. I lost customers. I lost stock. It was painful!

"Since then I learnt to put in hours interrogating key activities in all my business engagements. I thought through them and the ripple-effect they would create in the entire business model. I pondered how to execute the activities flawlessly and the necessary resources. And I looked out for obvious and hidden risks. I had no choice but to do things that way."

"And it worked well," John said in a statement of affirmation rather than a question.

"Be the judge. The point is—never get into a business model you have not figured out its critical activities for success." He went on to explain that the various building blocks in a business model require certain resources to work. These resources come in forms such as finance, people, skills, services, hardware, software, suppliers, partners, contractors and more, depending on the business type.

John recalled the assets test in the Wise Choice Criteria. Oscar confirmed that what V.J. called assets could as well be termed key resources. One needed to go through every aspect of the model and consider all the resources one required.

———

Oscar moved to the next building block. John was taking notes at a great speed. Over time, he had refined his note-taking skills and had even adopted one from the internet. It engaged all his mental faculties and captured points for further research and study. He understood that gurus provided room for student discovery. He remembered what one of his lecturer's mantras was: my work is to give you 5%, 95% is up to you!

Key Costs

Oscar took it from there. He said, "John, this is fundamental. All the building blocks incur costs. Most people get into businesses without exhaustively considering the costs, only to be rudely shocked along the way. Costs eat into profitability. Costs affect the affordability of a product or service. Costs affect competitiveness. Costs affect survivability. Any costs unknown will negatively impact any business.

"When it comes to costs, you better err on the side of over-projection. It is human nature to underestimate the costs and risks."

John nodded knowingly because he had experienced it. Online research had taught him that this mental condition was referred to by psychologists as *Optimism Bias*. It was a case where *new business idea excitement* led to *positive outcomes projection.* The focus was thus placed on low costs, zero imagined risks of failure, open and ready market, forecasted massive profits and speedy growth.

Oscar said, "That is a mental condition that propels entrepreneurs to move leaps and bounds. Whereas this is necessary for the economy, in the long run costs and risks should never be assumed.

"Costs come in two forms: variable and fixed. I don't know how business schools define those terms, but for me variable costs change with the number of products you sell, the services you deliver or the customers you serve.

"Fixed costs are incurred regardless, as long as you are in business. They are high-risk, especially for a start-up. They are one of the major reasons attributed to start-up failures. You are likely to incur fixed costs when you have too much money."

"Really?" John's voice hinted concern for the many entrepreneurs who incurred major fixed costs even before they got their first customer.

John was happy his business had minimal fixed costs. He knew of someone who blew all his start-up capital in weekly fresh flowers, full-time employees and expensive office furniture. He later felt validated to keep his fixed costs low.

Oscar lingered on the subject and seemed to enjoy it; probably because he was a manufacturer whose every penny spent meant significant implications.

He said, "Let me give you an example, John. In bar soaps business, the brands' price difference was three shillings. A shilling more incurred instantly meant a 33% profit loss. This translated to Kenya shillings one hundred million or sixty million in profit per annum.

"So, before you incur any fixed cost, question if it can be converted into a variable cost. This applies to rent and salaries, software and equipment costs, among other fixed assets. If it is an asset, interrogate if the business could run without necessarily owning it. The same is true in human resources. Would a skill be best hired or consulted on a need-basis?"

"Makes sense," John said.

"It does. But let me explain it further. There are costs you incur to acquire an asset that you would use over a long period and costs that you incur to consume a service. In the former you pay then you consume the service. In the latter you only pay for what you consume.

"Many business people use the former as way to show off on how well they are doing. They want people to talk of the vehicles, machinery, land and buildings they have acquired. While owning any of these assets, in and of itself, is not wrong, it might make a great idea become too expensive to execute and prolong the time it takes to make a profit.

Assets should never be acquired for show-off. Most entrepreneurs fall into this temptation. They are vanities if they are not needful.

"And by the way, John, do you know why I'm not a farmer?"

John shook his head. "Tell me."

"I don't want to incur all my costs before I have a specific order. I also don't want to be in a business in which I have minimal control of costs. That's why."

John knew what that meant. His parents had been farmers. The costs of inputs varied between planting and harvesting, depending on the vagaries of nature. He pitied farmers even though he appreciated their hard work and role in feeding the nation. Oscar saw him lost in thought and read it as his cue to move the discussion along.

He said, "Making money is the reason one gets into business."

John picked the sudden switch and sat up straight. "Did you say making money?"

Oscar nodded. "That is the basis of the next building block of the business model. Let's take another quick break then come back to it…"

———

Revenues

And come back to it they did. As soon as they sat, Oscar said, "You may call this the revenue model. It addresses the channels of generating revenue from your business. Are you going to make money from selling a product, upgrades, service parts, or a service? Are you going to sell subscriptions? Are you going to rent? Are you going to combine many forms of generating revenue? A great business has many channels, not just one, of generating revenue."

Oscar pulled out a card and placed it on the table. John stole a glance and saw a definition:

> A revenue model is a designed system through which a business converts its products and services into money—paid by the customer.

"Let me give you time to look at this diagram first," Oscar said as he gave the card to John. "It will help you discover hidden money in your business. It could also compel you to change the money-making strategies of your current services. I have seen people use the new tactic of offering a service free, thereby focusing on another more profitable area without changing their business entirely. But first, look at the diagram."

Some Revenue Models

1. Sell products and charge for service e.g restaurant;
2. Lease out the product e.g lease out an asset for a period of time ;
3. Charge for usage of a product;
4. Give a basic product for free and charge for additional features and capabilities like it happens for many games and software products;
5. Monetize your traffic e.g. through advertisements, displays and sampling;
6. Charge for usage licenses for support and updates on the product;
7. Buy and Sell for a Margin;
8. Buy, Enhance then sell at a premium;
9. Create a place where buyers and sellers meet then charge either one or both of them for the service;
10. Give a product for free then sell the consumables that go with the product e.g. giving a water dispenser then selling bottled water.

Illustration: Examples of Revenue Models

To Oscar's surprise, after John looked at the diagram, his first question was, "How do I price my services?" In his opinion he had set the right prices for his products, but the clientele had considered them too high, thus the struggle. Later, he ridiculously discounted his services.

John knew he wasn't alone in this. Many businesses, established as well as start-ups, floundered in setting right prices, making it one of the reasons many made losses. They had not mastered the art of getting their revenues to cover and exceed their costs, yet this was a basic lesson, the lesson that every business objective is to make profit. How did it elude folk? He wondered how even businesses ran by intelligent MBA graduates made losses. How was that even possible?

"Let me say this," Oscar said in answer to his question. "You will need to know all your costs. Ensure prices cover all other costs. Include both fixed and variable costs then set an acceptable profit margin. Afterwards, consider the premium value of the product, customers' ability to buy, and prices of similar products in the market. Remember that the ultimate test of a good price is the willingness of customers to pay for it. I urge you to do research and make your own pricing decisions."

John was disappointed. He had hoped for a magical answer. Then Oscar made a strange proposal. "Maybe you need to double your fees and triple your value. The customers may fight not to pay the price at first, but may later consider it a bargain."

John's eyes narrowed. "Are you serious?"

"Let me share with you my favourite revenue models. I prefer models that once I acquire a client I earn his money from repeated purchases over the client's lifetime. I don't engage in any model where each day I have to acquire a new customer to make more money."

"I get it," John said.

"Then we should get to the next building block, but before we do, don't forget that you make money only if your overall cash inflows exceed cash outflows. This means the money you receive from customers should exceed the money you spend creating and delivering value to them."

——

"The last building block covers business growth. It is key, unless you start a business without a plan to grow it. The model you choose affects how you scale up the business. You don't want to take a model that will make it hard to grow business. For example, if you became a business consultant, beware of the risk of building a practice around yourself as a person. It will greatly limit growth. You become the plant that cannot be easily replicated. You can build around ideas, systems and processes that can be patented, taught, franchised or even licensed. To understand this, look at a women's hospital compared to a clinic ran by the best gynecologist. The clinic is hard to replicate because it runs on the name and expertise of the doctor, while a hospital can be replicated many times over, including by fresh graduates."

Oscar's phone rang, but he ignored it.

"A remarkable difference between businesses that thrive and the ones that struggle is their design right from inception. Initial planning shapes the future. Sometimes entrepreneurs are comfortable with small beginnings before launching into deeper waters. It is important to create a business model that will accelerate the desired growth from the start. Behind that card, there are a few ways you may think about as you consider a design for business growth."

John turned the card.

As he looked at it, Oscar got up. He was running late for the next appointment. They agreed to meet after four days. By then John would have reviewed the business models and come to grips with them.

CHAPTER 13

PLANS ARE WORTHLESS, PLANNING IS ESSENTIAL

The waiter laid the table for the special Monday Blues Buster breakfast. John laid his business model canvas with notes written in different pen colours. He took Oscar through, highlighting the various unique points that indicated how different the business would be compared to its current state. Oscar could see he had done his homework and his excitement levels were through the roof.

John said, "Look, Oscar, my customer base has to be different. I used to target anyone who needed a website, but from now on I intend to focus only on professional service providers such as lawyers, doctors, architects, surveyors and management consultants. The key value for them would be how to get them more clients through internet marketing. What do you think?"

Oscar was impressed.

"This is better than doing a business plan," John said.

Suddenly Oscar became pensive in a way John had never seen before. He said, "John, let's enjoy this breakfast before I shock you to death."

It was neither a command nor a request. It sounded like a warning. John obliged. The breakfast was rich in protein and he wanted to enjoy it before he wowed Oscar with other great ideas he had gleaned from the card and other books he had been reading. Oscar looked at John and fixed his stern gaze on John.

But John couldn't help himself. He was itching to talk. He said, "I have zero respect for business plans, Oscar, especially for a new business or idea."

Oscar looked him in the eye and said nothing.

There was silence.

Again John couldn't help himself. He said, "A business plan, they say, is the most important document for an entrepreneur." He had heard that repeatedly. It was what he had learnt in his entrepreneurship class in college. It was a prerequisite document in banks for a business loan. It was also what consultants charged an arm and a leg to write. *We need to talk about this now,* he thought, looking at Oscar quizzically.

Oscar, for the first time, engaged. "Have you ever heard that the failure rate of all businesses, whether they have a business plan or not, does not change?"

John was stunned. Was Oscar out of his mind? From the books and studies he had read, the main reason new businesses failed was lack of a business plan. *Maybe this guy didn't learn very much from V.J. after all,* he thought.

But Oscar didn't stop. "The only value a business plan has to a business is that it is a good document to use to solicit for funds from banks. Beyond that, it gives you a false sense of understanding of your business. It helps the bankers buy time before telling you off. If that was not the case, why do they fund so many businesses that have no business plans?

If they were honest, they would tell you they finance the person, not the business plan.

"In other words, John, if a business plan ever made a new business succeed, there would be millions of new businesses succeeding every day because there are business plan templates and business plan writing software for any type of business you care to think of."

John had a fairly good knowledge of these templates and software. He also knew of business consultants who made writing business plans a career.

"Let's get deeper into this," Oscar said. "Business plans are worthless, but planning is priceless. A business plan is a document. Planning is a process. A business plan, at best, is based on imaginations, wishes, assumptions and guesswork yet many businesses, whether they have business plans or not, are started in this manner. They are built on the hope that underlying assumptions are true.

"The guesses could be about who the customers are, what they want to buy, how they want to buy, what the needed resources are, and projected profits per unit sale among other hypotheses. But once in business those assumptions may not hold. Most times they do not. If an entrepreneur realizes this early enough and makes needed changes, the business may succeed. Unfortunately, most entrepreneurs go to battle with business facts and realities that don't jell with their imaginations and guesses until it is too late."

John was a culprit. He had done this for five years. His was a case of fighting reality with false assumptions held hostage by a business plan.

"So do you see why it doesn't make any difference whether one has a business plan or not?" Oscar asked.

John nodded reluctantly.

But Oscar knew he'd understood because he had recorded the conversation well. John was a good juggler who could eat, listen and take notes with his left hand.

He was left-handed, but his teachers had forced him to use his right hand. They'd wanted him to be *normal.* *Normal* was what everyone else did.

But after meeting V.J. it had dawned on John that his role models were abnormal. They never thought like everyone else and did not act like other people. This made him argue that if success was born out of being normal, the world would be full of successful people. *But it is not, soo normal people were the probl...!*

Oscar interrupted his thoughts. "John, what are you thinking?"

John shrugged and left it at that.

"Then listen," Oscar said. "Validating your guesses and assumptions in the real world is the next stage in becoming a successpreneur. It is the next step in the planning process."

John got up. As he stretched, he thought of the words of Dwight Eisenhower:

The plan is useless, but planning is essential.

He wanted to ask Oscar what the military man turned president had in mind when he said these words, but when he looked at Oscar, he thought twice and let the man go. *So grouchy today he is,* John thought.

———

When Oscar got back he was aware the time they had was limited, so he got right to it. He declared to John that, "Everything you've been doing since you met V.J. is planning. If you had built your business on it, you are better placed than a person who built on a business plan. The difference is that you are designing a business archetype on paper rather than writing a document."

Archetype. Prototype. John was excited. He imagined himself designing a motor vehicle prototype, which if tested and was successful would be mass produced. The puzzle was solved.

So the purpose of the whole process was to create a business prototype? A prototype which could be replicated? It was a revelation!

Oscar's eyes narrowed. "This is the next step after coming up with the model. This is where you are testing and proving every imagination, assumption and guess in the market. You test whether the customer choice and product were right. You assess the revenue model. You investigate if the building blocks support each other. You want to be sure you have thought through all aspects of your business. It is time to get feedback from the real world."

Oscar pulled out another card. This one bad a quote from Steve Blank. It said: *This is the stage to take your idea out of the building.* John liked that. He promised himself he would read Steve Blank's books.

"At this stage, John, you have an opportunity to make necessary adjustments on any aspect of the idea or the business model according to the raw feedback, the responses, facts and realties you are getting from the market. Remember that the responses from the market are better than any data you can get through market research. This stage allows you to do away with the whole business model if you note that it does not work. You can decide to do away with the whole idea."

"What!"

Oscar's eyes narrowed again. "Yes, you can choose to make the business fail and walk away. Successpreneurs know they have a choice to fail by design, while others are forced out kicking and screaming!" He was graphic.

It means you can fail by design? John whispered loudly.

Oscar heard him and took the question on. "You can, though in reality it is not failing; you just prove that the idea or business model was inappropriate for the market. Knowing early saves you—as opposed to later, when a lot of investments have been made.

"However, this stage should not be overstretched. Despite the business model surviving, chances are you might need to adjust or discard it. Your goal here is not to survive and feel busy. It is not to hold on hoping for some unknown big break. It is to prove that the model can work. If it does not work, change it or kill it. The tragedy is that some businesses take too long to fail.

If it takes too long to die, sometimes you are better off killing it. There should be no shame at all in doing away with a business idea at this stage."

"What if it is the idea and business model I like? Do I have still to drop it and do something else?" John asked.

"If what you want is a hobby, don't drop it. If you want a business, the love of doing it and making of money must come together in a good business model. It is as simple as that, John."

———

"V.J. sends his regards," Oscar said as they resumed, after a break. "He had a successful surgery and is recovering well. He will be in hospital for another week or so. I will join him for that week and come back home with him. He asked me to remind you of your commitment and debt." They laughed.

"I can't wait to see him," John said, tears forming in his eyes. "He is such a great man, Oscar!"

"I miss him too, John, but let's leave that for a minute. I wanted to tell you that since I'll travel this weekend, we have only three days to finish the sessions. We will need to review your performance, then embark on the next stage of the programme," Oscar said.

"Sounds great!"

———

There was a sense that the sessions were coming to an end as the two gentlemen met again. The sessions had brought them so close that they had begun to feel a strong bond; the kind of connection only siblings could share. Maybe V.J. had succeeded in bringing together two sons, heirs of his great wisdom and entrepreneurial spirit. They got into the office and sat down.

"Why do we meet here?" John asked, pulling his chair to the edge so his arm could rest on the desk.

"Because business growth is the ultimate thing in business. If you don't get it right, you might as well shut down and do something else with your life!"

It sounded grim, but John sensed at once it needed to be so. *Business growth,* he thought silently. *Was that where I so remarkably failed?*

"Let's get started," Oscar said.

"I'm ready!"

"Once you prove that you have a workable business model, it is time to grow your business· This is the third stage in successpreneurship. It is the fun stage. The stage many entrepreneurs aspire to get to, including you; the stage where a business not only has a life of its own, but seems to be on an autopilot for growth.

"But let me back up a little so we can tie this in together later, okay? After the validating stage, you get a proven prototype that then becomes a start-up. This could become the next big thing. A start-up is the temporal state, where a business lays the stage for growth.

"It should not last one more day as a startup than it needs to. It should transition into a growth mode. This is deemed the most difficult transition for many entrepreneurs. It could explain the reason many businesses remain small. A majority of the so called Small and Medium sized Businesses (SMEs) are in this class. They remain SMEs for decades."

"Which is a shame, isn't it?" John asked.

"It is a big shame. At the startup stage, you need to be in control. But in a growing business, you later give up control and your role becomes leadership," Oscar said. He was supremely confident because he had built a number of successful businesses using these processes and had watched V.J. do the same.

To clear his doubts, John asked, "Is five years too long to be a star-up, Oscar?"

"The answer is yes. If you had a proven business model and got stuck, without any effort to transition into growth, there is a problem. My rule on all the businesses I have started is: if in two years we are unable to transition, we close down. It is up to each entrepreneur to make a logical decision based on the business they are in," Oscar said. "And by the way, at the stage of building a business, one needs to separate him or herself from the business. It should be an independent animal."

"Does that mean you register the business as a limited company?" John was not sure whether he intended that as a question or he was making a statement.

Oscar shook his head. "Far from it, John. I know it is what you were taught in business law, however, a business can be legally independent but still be one hundred percent dependent on you.

Legal independence only talks about the separation of the company and personal liabilities and obligations. They say that a legal company has a life of its own such that if you died the company would still run.

"But that does not happen for most companies. They do not survive beyond three years after a founder's death—and when the founding entrepreneur is sick they get sick. If *she* is on maternity leave, the company also takes a break." Oscar burst out laughing. "Get it?"

John cut the laughter short. "It's not funny, Oscar. That is my business we are talking about. If I broke my leg today, my business will hurt. I remember when Mama passed away and I got into a mourning period. I guess my business underwent the same, right?"

Oscar said, "My friend, business building is about getting out of that very kind of situation, a condition common among providers of professional services such as lawyers, management consultants, engineers and doctors. It takes a lot of time to train a professional. It takes time and effort to make a living from it. One needs to convert what he or she does into a business.

"In other words, John, when building a business you need to cut off the umbilical cord from yourself. You should start building processes and systems that create value and make money. These systems and processes should be independent of you and should be delegated to your best employees. As an owner, as much as you create the business systems and processes, they should be simple and easy to pass on to others."

John excused himself to the washroom. As he slipped out, Oscar called for tea. In the washroom, John quietly cried. The realization that he needed to drastically change hit him. The e-business consultancy that he had been so excited about would have ended the same way as his five-year long struggling business. *How many umbilical cords would I need to sustain the businesses*, he asked himself. It also became clear to him why some entrepreneurs built many businesses while some got so tired and overwhelmed to make one work. He returned to the table.

And Oscar didn't even wait for him to settle down. He said, "John, the process of building a business is what many people call working on your business instead of working in the business."

"Pardon me!" John did not catch what Oscar had just said. "Could you please repeat that?"

Oscar frowned. "John? Have you been crying?"

John looked down.

"What I said was—a wise entrepreneur works on his business, not in his business." He said it with the conviction of a Pentecostal preacher.

"Works on, not in," John repeated.

"That's right, John. This is what it means. When you work in your business you are the engine, the mind, the soul of the business. You have to be present for the business to work. You have to sell to get sales. You have to keep an eye on the till. You have to ensure people are working. In that kind of business, nothing moves unless you move.

"Working on your business means you create processes and procedures for doing things, set expected standards for routine tasks, and put in place systems to ensure that there is order in the business."

"Makes perfect sense," John said.

But Oscar wasn't done yet. "Let me use marketing to demonstrate. In my consumer products businesses, marketing is one of the key functions in the business. If I was working in the business, I would ensure that I make all the decisions that affect marketing. But what I have done is—I have processes and procedures in place that guide identification of profitable markets, growing markets and markets we need to get out of.

"When it comes to new product development, we have procedures and criteria that the businesses use for generation and evaluation. We have standards on how many products need to be introduced into the market every year. We have a criterion to use in evaluating our distribution channels. I don't need to be involved in deciding who will be our distributor and who should not. I built these systems in the initial stage."

John shook his head in disbelief. "How come I wasn't taught this in business school, Oscar?"

"Maybe it was taught when you were absent," Oscar said and laughed. He went on to ask John to focus on building the business prototype first. "I make you a promise, John. Once you have built the prototype, you and I will do the business building together. Do we have a deal?"

John agreed and left to make it happen!

EPILOGUE

AND IT CAME TO PASS

They laid V.J. to rest seven months after John had met him. V.J. battled like a true warrior. He died smiling. Oscar and John stood beside the grave without saying much. They would miss him, but his wisdom would live on. They were grateful that he had taught them business wisdom. They knew that seven months was a short time in business, but *applied wisdom* in the same timeframe had turned around his fortunes. John was done with the prototyping stage and was on his way to growth.

John was amused that Bank Money was now being offered incessantly. *When I started, they didn't think of me, but now that I am established, they chase me with all manner of propositions. My business plans have no longer become necessary,* he thought as he wondered at the ways of the world.

What pained him most, however, was that he had not won Michelle back. Seven months later, they had not resolved their differences. She had moved to another town after redeployment by her employer. They kept in touch and he saw the kids often, but it was gradually dawning on him that business success may not win him love after all. He was going to need a guru to teach him how to win back his wife!

———

"Now go fulfill your last promise to V.J." Oscar said.

John had to start putting together the wisdom into a book. A book that would help entrepreneurs become successpreneurs. He hoped the book would reach as many people as possible, especially those like him who had been trapped in hustling rather than creating and running businesses that would excel and outlive them.

NOTES AND DEFINITIONS

Please Note web links provided here were working at the time of writing the book. We cannot guarantee they will continue working. But using Search Engines you are likely to access most of them if the link fails.

NOTES

1. Jua Kali – This is a Swahili word referring to boutique businesses where the operators are self employed.
2. There has been a lot of debate on whether entrepreneurs are employable.
3. The first law of holes or Law of holes. Retrieved from
   http://en.wikipedia.org/wiki/First_law_of_holes
4. The Bible, John 8:32
5. Pausch, R. Professor of Computer Science, who said this quote in his last lecture. He knew that he would die soon and he decided to perform a final lecture, I advise to everyone watch this lecture, specially for improve motivation skills. Retrieved from
   https://www.youtube.com/watch?v=j7zzQpvoYcQ

6. The Kenyatta International Conference Centre (KICC) is a 28-story building located in <u>Nairobi</u>, Kenya. The KICC is located in the central business district of Nairobi . Retrieved from <u>http://en.wikipedia.org/wiki/Kenyatta_Internati onal_Conference_Centre</u>

7. Thousands of jobless people, men and women, young and old walk many kilometers every day from various slums to industrial areas in major Kenyan towns with a hope a getting a job for the day. Most of them end up not getting the casual job that pays the legal minimum wage for the day and will make the trip back home and the following day they come back again with a hope they will be lucky. **Retrieved from http://en.wikipedia.org/wiki/Tsavo_Man-Eaters**

8. **HTTP://EN.WIKIPEDIA.ORG/WIKI/VOI**

9. I recommend you read the articles Writing and Remembering: Why We Remember What We Write by <u>Dustin Wax</u> and <u>Why You Learn More Effectively by Writing Than Typing</u> by Melanie Pinola Life Hacker Website <u>http://www.lifehack.org/articles/productivity/ writing-and-remembering-why-we-remember-what-we-write.html</u>

http://lifehacker.com/5738093/why-you-learn-more-effectively-by-writing-than-typing

10. I strongly suggest you read the book *Heart, Smarts, Guts, and Luck* Anthony K. Tjan , Richard J. Harrington and Tsun-Yan Hsieh (HBR Press, 2012). You can also take a free entrepreneur aptitude test on the website by the authors http://www.hsgl.com/

11. Successpreneur is a term I have coined to describe an entrepreneur who has moved from hustling to following a process to create a successful business from his idea.

12. The distinction made between entrepreneurs and successpreneurs in this book is mainly to emphasize a point and in no way meant to be derogatory to the entrepreneurs.

13. Matatu. It is a fourteen seater or twenty five seater cab where the passengers split the bill. It is the Swahili word for public service transport vehicle.

14. Check out on cancer causes on this link http://www.cancer.gov/cancertopics/causes

15. Knowledge only creates potential for power. Its application is where the power is. A powerful quote by Tony Robbins, Speaker and Author. I highly recommend his books and tapes.

Retrieved from

16. I have created this pyramid of business needs in line with Maslow's Hierarchy of Human Motivations. We are still refining this concept.

17. Access not Ownership concept that most successful entrepreneurs are able to leverage well to create successful organizations.

18. Youth Fund and Women Fund are two funds ran by the government of Kenya to provide Financial support to entrepreneurs below age of thirty five and women respectively set up businesses.

19. This practice has changed my relationship with money. I recommend it to every entrepreneur who finds it difficult to pay his debts.

20. The understanding of business model concept has been heavily influenced by Steve Blank , Eric Ries and Alexander Osterwalder. I cannot do justice to the concept while trying to simplify and contextualize their teachings in this book. For those who may find the concept too simplified or complicated in this book I recommend you read the books they have authored Four Steps to Epiphany by Steve

Blank, <u>Business Model Generation</u> by Alexander Osterwalder, Lean Startup by Eric Ries.

The Business Model Canvas is a great tool to use in the process of developing your business model. Retrieved from http://www.businessmodelgeneration.com/downloads/business_model_canvas_poster.pdf Read more of the same from the website http://www.businessmodelgeneration.com

21. What is it that those who you consider more successful than you are doing that you are not doing?

22. Watch Tali Sharot Ted Talk on the subject of Optimism Bias. Retrieved from https://www.ted.com/talks/tali_sharot_the_optimism_bias . Tali is a Cognitive neuroscientist.

23. The website www.bmnow.com by Eran Laniado does a great job in listing and giving quick explanation on 26 common revenue models. Retrieved from http://www.bmnow.com/revenue-models-quick-guide/

24. There is no mind on business growth strategies I know of who is greater than Jay Abraham. He is not just a genius but a guru on application of his strategies. I recommend you read his book Getting Everything You Can Out of All You've

Got, Jay Abraham, 2000. Visit his website for more of what he does www.abraham.com

25. Cancer treatment types. Retrieved from http://www.cancer.org/treatment/treatmentsandsideeffects/treatmenttypes/

26. A Day Job Is So Much Easier Than Entrepreneurship.
Financial Samurai. Retrieved from http://www.financialsamurai.com/a-day-job-is-so-much-easier-than-entrepreneurship/

27. Profit can no longer be the only purpose. Future organizations must be both morally and socially responsible and profitable. Retrieved from http://www.taniaellis.com/wp-content/uploads/2011/11/The-Era-of-Compassionate-Capitalism.pdf

28. (AUGUST 2009).WALKING: YOUR STEPS TO HEALTH. THE HARVARD HEALTH PUBLICATION. RETRIEVED FROM HTTP://WWW.HEALTH.HARVARD.EDU/NEWSLETTERS/HARVARD MENS HEALTH WATCH/2009/AUGUST/WALKING-YOUR-STEPS-TO-HEALTH

29. An Infographic on why businesses fail. Retrieved from http://www.byreputation.com/Small-Business-Success_a/560.htm

30. New Research Finds Business Plans Are Virtually Useless. Advice to Entrepreneurs: Perfect the Business, Not the Business Plan. Retrieved from https://www.equitynet.com/blog/wp-content/uploads/2011/08/Article-Business-Plans-are-Virtually-Useless-Univ-of-Maryland.pdf

REFERENCES

Anthony, K. T. (May 16, 2012). Great Businesses don't start With a Plan generates a lot of discussion this subject. Retrieved from http://blogs.hbr.org/2012/05/great-businesses-dont-start-wi/

Bach, R. (2006). Jonathan Livingston Seagull.

Blair, R. (May 23, 2013). Why Business Plans Are Worthless. Forbes Magazine. *RYAN IS THE CEO OF* <u>ViSalus</u>, *A SERIAL ENTREPRENEUR AND #1 NEW YORK TIMES BESTSELLING AUTHOR OF* "<u>Nothing to Lose, Everything to Gain: How I Went from Gang Member to Multimillionaire Entrepreneur</u>". *YOU CAN DOWNLOAD A SAMPLE CHAPTER OF HIS BOOK HERE* Retrieved from http://ryanblair.com/book.php

BLAKESLEE, S. (April 2, 2012). Mind Games: Sometimes a White Coat Isn't Just a White Coat, New York Times. Retrieved from http://www.nytimes.com/2012/04/03/science/clothes-and-self-perception.html

BLANK, S. (2013). THE FOUR STEPS TO THE EPIPHANY.

Brendan, C. (May 7, 2012). Business Plans Don't Work. Retrieved from http://www.innovationexcellence.com/blog/2012/05/07/business-plans-dont-work/

BRENT, B. (May 13, 2009). Investors Pay Business Plans Little Heed. The New York Times. Retrieved from http://www.nytimes.com/2009/05/14/business/smallbusiness/14hunt.html?_r=0

Carlson, R. (1997). Don't Sweat the Small Stuff...and It's All Small Stuff.

Carol, J. S, Donald, H. S . Dressing for success: Effects of color and layering on perceptions of women in business.

Covey, S. (1989). The Seven Habits of Highly Effective People. Explains the idea of being proactive rather than reactive. He has well demonstrated this using two circles.

Foer, J. (June 11, 2012). How to train your mind to remember anything. Retrieved from http://www.cnn.com/2012/06/10/opinion/foer-ted-memory/ Watch Joshua Foer *the author of "Moonwalking with Einstein: The Art and Science of Remembering Everything." Giving a Ted Talk on how the brain works in 2005* **http://www.ted.com/talks/neil burgess how your brain tells you where you are**

Gladwell, M. (November 18, 2008). Outliers: The Story of Success.

Henderson, L.M. (March 30, 2012). Freedom and Prosperity. The Compassionate Capitalist.

Johnson, K.P. and lennon, S. The Social Psychology of Dress: A Bibliographic Guide. Retrieved from http://www.bergfashionlibrary.com/page/The%20Social%20Psychology%20of%20Dress

Kate, L. (January 2011). Myth of the Business Plan : Writing one is largely a joke. The Entrepreneur Magazine. Retrieved from http://www.entrepreneur.com/article/217768

KOLSTAD, I & WIIG, A. (SEPTEMBER 2011).EDUCATION AND ENTREPRENEURIAL SUCCESS. RETRIEVED FROM HTTPS://WWW.TCD.IE/ECONOMICS/ASSETS/PDF/ENTREPRENEURSHIP_AND_EDUCATION_DUBLIN.PDF

Maslow, A. H. (1943). A Theory of Human Motivation. Retrieved from http://psychclassics.yorku.ca/Maslow/motivation.htm

MICHAEL, E. G. (OCTOBER 14, 2004). THE E-MYTH REVISITED: WHY MOST SMALL BUSINESSES DON'T WORK AND WHAT TO DO ABOUT IT. **Another great book on this subject is** Work the System: The Simple Mechanics of Making More & Working Less , Sam Carpenter, 3rd Edition

Napoleon, H. (1938). Think and Grow Rich.

Peck, S. M. (1978). The Road Less Traveled.

Peter, H. (November 8, 2010). Death by business planning? Retrieved from http://simventure.co.uk/wordpress/business-planning/

SHAPIRO, F.R., EDITOR. (2006). THE YALE BOOK OF QUOTATIONS. JOSEPH EPSTEIN (FOREWORD)

Smith, P.S. Types of business resources slides . The Science of Start – Types of resources. Retrieved from http://www.slideshare.net/PaulShawSmith/061-types-of-resources

Szalavitz, M. (Sept. 06, 2011). The Secrets of Self-Control: The Marshmallow Test 40 Years Later. Time Magazine.

THORIN, K. (DECEMBER 14, 2011). DRESS FOR SUCCESS WITH SCIENCE. RETRIEVED FROM HTTP://LIFEHACKER.COM/5867952/DRESS-FOR-SUCCESS-WITH-SCIENCE

Whitford, D. (March 30, 2011). Can compassionate capitalists really win? Fortune Magazine. Retrieved from http://fortune.com/2011/03/30/can-compassionate-capitalists-really-win/

Dear Sam,

Re: The Guy Who Cracked the Code

My business development eyes opened the day I finished reading your book: **The Guy Who Fired His Boss.** Am so grateful that God brought this up at the perfect moment when I am trying to turn around my struggling business. The main character in the book is in a similar situation like I am in currently. But in the book I find inspiration and encouragement.

The step by step lessons have been instrumental in the planning process am currently in. This has also been facilitated by a white paper report you wrote sometime back; ***Prison Break: 7 Top constraints that hinder SMEs Growth into Big Companies.*** This has helped me understand my business in a way I have never understood before. The one thing I have difficulty cracking is: What the best business model for our business is. My one request, could you be my V.J as I get into the process of discovering it?

As I went through *The Guy Who Fired His Boss* I realized what I did wrong from day one: having no definite problems to solve, a not-thought-out business model, undefined target market, haphazard and costly marketing and working in the business instead of working on it. Am grateful that I have learnt this now.

Now am on the road to success. It is clear on my mind how I will go about connecting the dots as I transition from an entrepreneur into a Successpreneur. The distinction between the two is like mid-day and mid-night.

I'm charged and inspired to share these lessons with fellow youngpreneurs in my circle. I would also love to support your cancer initiative. I'm happy I have discovered you and your work.

Thank you for the wonderful book.

Best Regards,

Denis Gachoki

Coming Soon By Same Author

1. The Velvet Rope

     ~This book is about how to get people to buy the first time and keep them buying again and again.

2. Street Smart Selling

     ~This is a book on common sense approaches to selling, the kind of approaches your professors won't teach you in the business school.

Other Great Books By
Sahel Publishing Association

1. *Unleash Your Full Potential*, by George Wachiuri
2. *The Doctrine of Strategic Planning*, by Dr. Edward Odundo
3. *Remember*, by Dr. Vincent Orinda
4. *Walking On The Edge,* by Joe Muchekehu
5. *Transformed To Transform*, by Peter Muya Hamisi
6. *Understanding Arthritis*, by Dr. Omondi Oyoo
7. *The Dance Party,* by K.B. Onyango
8. *Listen Little Children,* by Lillian Omuga
9. *Heal Our Land,* by Sam Okello
10. *Raisng A Healthy Child,* by Petronila Muthoni Agwata
11. *Soaring Like An Eagle,* by George Wachiuri
12. *Luo Kitgi Gi Timbegi E Ngima Masani,* by PLO Lumumba

There will be many more books that will answer life's toughest questions for you, because as we always say, Sahel Publishing Association's promise is: Books That Speak To Your Hopes and Fears. Call us today**: 0715.596.106 or 0731.651.927**. Talk to one of Africa's most-sought ghostwriters and editors, Hon Sam Okello, about your writing dreams!

Visit any of our authors at: www.amazon.com
Our website: www.sahelpublishing,net
We are in Kenya, the U.S.A., The U.K. and India

Publish your book with us today!

Make Notes Here:

-